32. DAIRY

Toys & Games

THE SMITHSONIAN ILLUSTRATED LIBRARY OF ANTIQUES

General Editor: Brenda Gilchrist

Toys & Games

William C. Ketchum, Jr.

COOPER-HEWITT MUSEUM

The Smithsonian Institution's National Museum of Design

ENDPAPERS
Prints for a Zoetrope. English, late nineteenth century.
Cooper-Hewitt Museum, gift of Mrs. Dexter J. Purinton

FRONTISPIECE
A Pollock's theater set for a play, lithographed paper and
cardboard. Toy theaters were especially popular in England,
and each one contained the figures and costumes for a specific
London production. English, late nineteenth century. Cooper-
Hewitt Museum, gift of W. H. Solle

Art Direction, Design: JOSEPH B. DEL VALLE

Contents

1 Introduction

Of all antiques, toys are perhaps the most evocative. They bear a legacy of fragile memory and passion. It is certainly possible for even the best-intentioned outsider to view with indifference a Queen Anne tall chest or a piece of Georgian silver, but few remain unaffected at the sight of a battered Teddy bear or a dented tin train. These are the very stuff of our lives, and every one of them reminds us of toys we once owned or wished to own. Small wonder that toy collecting, though of rather recent vintage (most public and private collections were not begun until the twentieth century), has become a major hobby in North America, western Europe and Japan.

An added reason for our great interest in toys is that many of them were directly related to the adult life of the period in which they were manufactured, and thus have important social and historical significance. In some cases this is evident from the playthings themselves. Dolls were not only dressed to resemble their young owners and their owners' mothers but sometimes even had period hairdos, so that it is possible to date them quite accurately from coiffure alone. Cast-iron toys were frequently based on real-life prototypes—in this case, the trains and wheeled vehicles that transformed transportation at the turn of the century.

But the social implications of toys go beyond these obvious bounds. They strongly reflect accepted contemporary mores—that little boys should be brave, honest and hardworking, that little girls should be kind, dutiful and attentive to their elders. And they reflect, too, the prejudices that existed at the time they were produced. Games like "Alabama Coon" and mechanical banks denominated "Paddy and His Pig" or "Chinese Must Go" reveal such feelings all too clearly.

In part, a toy's fidelity to life was intended to please children eager to mimic their elders; but to a greater extent it indicated the preferences of parents. Prior to the nineteenth century, life for most

Colorplate 1.
Optical toy, "Les Anamorphoses," steel shaft with a mirror finish, lithographed, hand-tinted images. When viewed in the steel tube, the distorted images assume a realistic appearance. French, Paris, c. 1865, published by Jullien. Cooper-Hewitt Museum, purchased in memory of Norvin Hewitt Green

people was very difficult, and childhood was a luxury few adults could afford to indulge. Children were regarded as miniature grown-ups and were expected to get through their formative years as quickly as possible so that they might assume their roles in the "real" world. This meant strict discipline, a strong religious background and scholars who entered Harvard at age eleven. It also resulted in toys that were perceived as training tools: board games and books with a religious or social message, dollhouses and model kitchens to inculcate the arts of housewifery, even hobbyhorses to acquaint the potential knight with the dangers of an unruly mount. Of course, there was some free time, and it can be guessed at from the toys that served no evident social purpose. Kites, hoops, balls and jack straws were used to while away the idle hours of an all-too-fleeting childhood.

As collectors' items, toys differ from other antiques in that most of the objects are not of any great age. The few "toys" found at Egyptian, Greek, Roman and medieval sites are practically unattainable to the collector. Even during the seventeenth and eighteenth centuries, playthings were too expensive for the general population, and few examples have survived. Not until the Industrial Revolution, with its improvements in methods of manufacturing and its spawning of a working class with some money to spend, do we see the results of a widespread manufacture of toys.

Certainly, most examples before the nineteenth century were individually handmade, usually of wood, clay or metal, though the rich might have silver or porcelain, and paper was not unknown. During the first half of the nineteenth century such innovations in machinery as the jigsaw, chromolithography and the adoption of a crude assembly line finally made it possible for manufacturers to turn out toys in sufficient volume to sell them for relatively little. These developments also made it possible to establish an export trade.

But the great bulk of collectible toys date to the late nineteenth and early twentieth centuries, when production techniques allowed for an output ranging into the thousands and even millions of units, thus ensuring a reasonably large number of survivals. Most of these objects, including some of the finest, such as mechanical banks and board games, are truly creatures of the factory age—untouched by human hands. To certain collectors, this is just fine. They seek out the factory-made toys as important signs of industrialization and the coming of a modern age, and are not at all interested in the hand-formed playthings that less well-to-do mothers and fathers continued to make into this century. These homemade pieces, which have come to be known as folk toys or even folk art, are currently in great demand.

Whatever one's preference, there are toys to be found. One of the most attractive aspects of the field is that so many examples are available to the average collector. Items in certain areas, such as early tin and cast-iron toys, are quite expensive, but it is also possible to obtain reasonably priced examples. Most important, every one of these playthings will have a poignant story to tell and vivid memories to evoke.

2   The Earliest Toys

While there can be little doubt that toys of one sort or another have existed as long as there were children to enjoy them, early examples are both rare and problematical. The ephemeral nature of playthings has limited the number that have survived; and those toylike objects that have been found, chiefly in tombs and at the sites of ruined cities, may not always be what they appear. We know that the great number of miniature figures and household objects found in Egyptian tombs were intended not as toys but as ritual offerings, designed to accompany the deceased into a new world. The same may be said of the earthenware figures of soldiers and horses (*Haniwa*) uncovered in Japanese graves of the fourth century B.C.

Yet the highly advanced state of Egyptian, Greek and Roman societies presupposes the existence of a small elite with the free time necessary for the amusement of children and adults alike, and there is no doubt that toys and games were manufactured in those days. Playing cards date to at least the fourteenth century, while dice or the variation known as knucklebones have been found in pre-Christian graves. As early as the reign (c. 1801–1792 B.C.) of Amenemhet IV, the Egyptians were amusing themselves with elaborate board games such as one dubbed "Hounds and Jackals" (plate 1).

The graves of Egyptian children have been found to contain dolls, made either of carved wood (plate 2) or of linen stuffed with bunches of papyrus, and the Nile dwellers were familiar with a version of the modern-day pull toy. Wooden models of tigers and horses believed to be nearly three thousand years old were found during excavations at Thebes. The Egyptians could even boast of crude mechanical toys—ivory animals with articulated jaws designed so that by moving an attached rod, one could make the creatures appear to bark or growl (colorplate 2).

Colorplate 2.
Mechanical toy in the form of a dog, carved ivory. Movement of the rod causes the dog's jaws to open. Egyptian, Eighteenth Dynasty (c. 1570–1293 B.C.). Metropolitan Museum of Art, New York, Rogers Fund, 1940

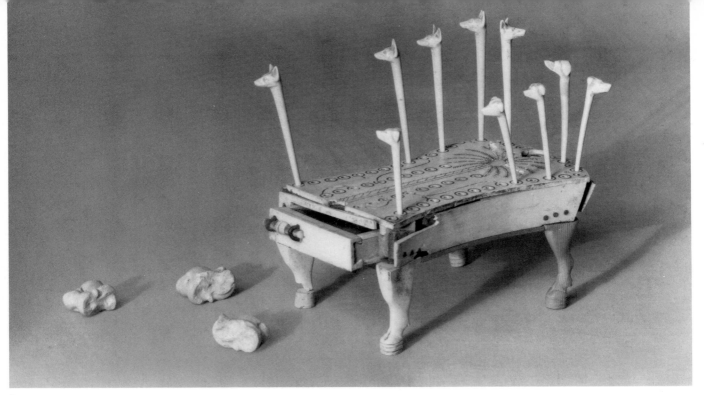

1

Many of the small pieces found in ancient grave sites are made of clay; they include animals and tiny cooking and eating utensils, as well as accurate representations of contemporary homes and their furnishings. Most of these were probably of religious importance. But the earthenware horses and chariots from the fifth or fourth century B.C. discovered in Greece, mounted on platforms with wheels, are most likely a form of pull toy. Similarly mobile figures of Persian origin, carved from stone, have been found dating back to 1100 B.C.

Horses were, of course, very important in those societies fortunate enough to possess them, and both the hobbyhorse and the pull-toy version are of great antiquity. A Greek pull-toy horse cut in silhouette from a single plank of wood, with a hole drilled through its nose to receive a rein or drawstring, was found during excavation of a structure dating to 400 B.C., and Sung dynasty ceramics bear representations of Chinese children riding hobbyhorses (plate 3). European literary references indicate that hobbyhorses were used (as they would be during the medieval period) to instruct boys in the rudiments of horsemanship.

The Greeks and the Romans also had dolls. Some were of clay, but Roman rag dolls from the fourth century A.D. are known. The children of Rome played with stone or glass marbles (plate 4) and with kites—an Asiatic invention brought back by traders. No doubt other types of playthings also existed, but it is evident even from these survivals that the children of the ancients were reasonably well supplied with toys.

Much less is known of the Dark Ages that followed the final disintegration of the western Roman Empire. The chaos of the times

2

1.
Game of "Hounds and Jackals," in ivory
with ebony veneer. Gambling and board
games such as this appear in the earliest
cultures. Egyptian, c. 1801–1786 B.C. Metropolitan Museum of Art, New York,
Carnarvon Collection, gift of Edward S.
Harkness, 1926

2.
Doll, carved wood. Small human replicas like
this are found in the remains of various an-
cient societies. Egyptian, c. 2160–1788 B.C.
Metropolitan Museum of Art, New York,
Carnarvon Collection, gift of Edward S.
Harkness, 1926

3

3.
Pillow, slip-glazed pottery (Tz'u Chou ware).
The figure of the boy riding a hobbyhorse
is one of the earliest-known representations of this popular toy. Chinese, Sung
dynasty (A.D. 960–1279). Metropolitan Museum of Art, New York, Harris Brisbane
Dick Fund, 1960

4.
Marbles, mosaic glass, varying in size from
½ to 2 in. (1.2 to 5 cm.) in diameter. The
game of marbles has changed very little over
the centuries. Roman, fourth century A.D.
Metropolitan Museum of Art, New York

4

was conducive neither to relaxation nor to the preservation of delicate objects like toys, and the writings of the period give us little hint as to the activities of the young. With the establishment of the feudal order, however, toys once more appeared. There are medieval German woodcuts showing boys playing with models of jousting knights, and from thirteenth-century Magdeburg come metal figures of soldiers and civilians, which may have been the first military miniatures or nothing more than decorative ornaments.

Excavations in England have yielded small-scale fourteenth-century bronze and pewter utensils, and hobbyhorses are pictured in a French Book of Hours from the same era. These medieval hobbyhorses consisted of a carved head or head and upper body mounted on a stick to which leather reins were attached—a form that remained basically unchanged until the twentieth century.

We can assume that the hobbyhorse was intended entirely for the amusement of children, but other popular medieval games were played by young and old alike. One of the best known was stick and ball, or bilboquet. A pierced ball was attached by a cord to a rod that had a tapered or cuplike ending. Contestants threw the ball into the air and attempted to catch it either in the cup or on the spike. Sixteenth-century French prints depict groups of children and adults playing at bilboquet, and it is likely that the game is much older. Wooden cups and balls were generally decorated with paint, but the finest examples were of ivory, richly carved and inscribed (colorplate 3).

Another game of ancient lineage is battledore and shuttlecock, a form of early badminton played with oval wooden paddles and a feathered "bird," or shuttlecock. This pastime is shown in medieval European prints and paintings, and was equally popular during both ancient and more recent times in Japan, where the battledore was called a *hagoita* (colorplate 4).

Not all early games were designed for the athletically inclined. Gambling of various kinds seems to have been popular among Euro-

Colorplates 3 & 4.

Left: Stick and ball toy (bilboquet), ivory, carved and decorated. Bilboquet appears to be a simple game, but considerable dexterity is required to catch the ball. French, late eighteenth century. Cooper-Hewitt Museum, anonymous gift

Right: Battledore (*hagoita*), wood, painted and gilded. Battledore and shuttlecock was a game popular in both East and West. Japanese, probably seventeenth to eighteenth century. Tokyo National Museum

5.
Game token or counter, carved ivory. Small animal figures were used as counters in several Eskimo games. Alaskan, St. Lawrence Island, c. 1100–1300. Private collection

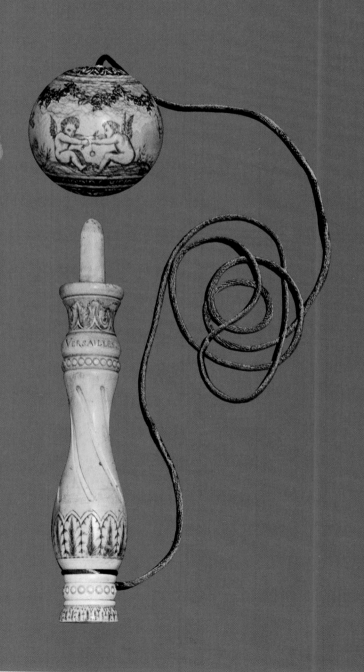

COLORPLATE 5

peans and Asiatics, and even with relatively primitive societies such as the Eskimo of western Alaska, where men carved ivory animals to serve as counters (plate 5).

Dolls continued much in evidence in castle and keep, with the English making wooden examples as early as the fourteenth century, although these appear to have been "fashion" dolls, designed to illustrate clothing styles, and may not have been intended for play. In the fifteenth century there were also paper figures that could be suspended above a stove or fireplace, where they might move and flutter in the updraft; again, these novelties were probably intended as much for the amusement of adults as of children. Excavation of a burial pit near London has brought to light a tiny Gothic-style rocking chair dating to the reign (1625–49) of Charles I, and fourteenth-century doll furnishings have been uncovered near Jena in Germany.

Amusement was no doubt very much on the mind of the creator of another early toy, the coral and bells. This multipurpose piece was definitely meant for very young children. It consisted of a whistle (usually made of silver) attached to a bell-hung centerpiece of the same material and terminating in a piece of pink coral. The coral and bells could thus serve both as toy and teething ring. But the device had a further significance, since it appears in paintings and etchings from medieval Europe in a clearly talismanic role. As late as the eighteenth century, coral and bells were given as christening presents in the hope that they might ward off illness—as long as the coral did not fade, the little owner would remain in good health. Most coral and bells, like their eventual successors, the "pearl" and silver teething rings, were made of precious metals (plate 6), although gold examples (colorplate 5) are rare.

The toys and games described here must represent only a small portion of those in existence during the thousands of years of human childhood on earth. Yet they encompass most of the categories—dolls, pull toys, military figures, board games and sports equipment—into which modern playthings may be divided. Moreover, the very longevity of certain items, such as hobbyhorses and marbles, indicates that the tastes and desires of children and their parents have changed surprisingly little over the years.

Colorplate 5.
Coral and bells, gold and pink coral. It is uncommon for this toy to be found in gold. American, mid-eighteenth century. Metropolitan Museum of Art, New York, Rogers Fund, 1947

6.
Left: Coral and bells in silver and pink coral, English, c. 1840. *Right:* Teething ring in silver and mother-of-pearl, American, c. 1870. The coral and bells combined bell, whistle and teething ring. Its less complex successor appeared in the late nineteenth century. Both, Cooper-Hewitt Museum, gift of Mrs. Max Farrand

Colorplate 6.
Noah's ark, wood, carved and painted.
Carved arks and their accompanying figures
(which may number in the hundreds) were
traditional Christmas gifts. German, c. 1915.
Margaret Woodbury Strong Museum,
Rochester, New York

3 Wooden Playthings

It seems likely that the first objects with which children amused themselves were made of wood, and there can be no doubt that until the mid-nineteenth century the great majority of all toys were constructed from this material.

Small carved figures, both animal and human, have a long though generally anonymous history. Since they were rarely signed by their creators, it is often difficult to distinguish early examples from those carved at a much later date. A few of the craftsmen are known, though. One was Wilhelm Schimmel (c. 1817–1890), who worked in Pennsylvania's Cumberland County. Schimmel's pieces include farm animals, human figures, birds, squirrels and dogs (plate 7).

Carvings of this sort are likely to appear in almost any culture and at any time, but Germany seems to have been a particularly prolific source. As early as the 1700s, craftsmen in the Berchtesgaden and Sonneberg regions of the country were shaping and painting small animals that were transported to Nuremberg for distribution. Known as "Nuremberg Ware" in the trade, these inexpensive toys were shipped throughout the Western world. Initially carved in the round, a century later such pieces were being roughed out on a lathe and then hand-finished.

Ranging in size from a few inches to several feet, carved animals might be played with as individual pieces or assembled in groups. The first such grouping, for the traditional Christmas crèche, appeared at least as early as 1400. Farmyard arrangements were also popular, and with the importation of exotic animals came the first toy zoos. Most interesting to the collector are the Noah's arks (color-plate 6), some of which may include over a hundred different pieces. The earliest existent arks date to the seventeenth century, but the great majority were made in northern Europe and North America over the past one hundred and fifty years.

7.
Folk-art toys, carved and painted wood: *top*, squirrel; *bottom*, dog. Handmade playthings of this sort were produced until late in the nineteenth century. Made by Wilhelm Schimmel. American, Pennsylvania, c. 1860–70. New-York Historical Society, New York City

8.
Jointed figure of Felix the Cat, lathe-turned and painted wood. During the 1920s and 1930s, toys based on comic strip figures became extremely popular. A. Schoenhut Company. American, Philadelphia, Pennsylvania, c. 1927. Margaret Woodbury Strong Museum, Rochester, New York

Related to these earlier examples is the popular factory-made "Humpty Dumpty Circus," and the other figures produced in the early twentieth century by the firm of Albert Schoenhut, a German immigrant who founded his own business in Philadelphia in 1872. Lathe-turned and hand-painted, these figures (colorplate 7 and plate 8) are jointed so that they can be placed in various positions.

Perhaps the most popular of all carved toys is the horse. Reference has already been made to very early hobbyhorses; enthusiasm for the beast did not diminish with the passage of time. Rocking horses were widely made in Europe and North America during the eighteenth and nineteenth centuries. Indeed, it is sometimes difficult to distinguish a Continental example from one made in America. The earliest rocking horses consisted of broad plank rockers (each of which looked rather like half a pie), surmounted by a carved head or head and upper body, while later examples were fully carved and mounted on long, curved rockers (plate 9). There were other variants as well, including the *shoofly*, a seat arranged within two saw-cut outlines of horses (colorplate 8) and the *velocipede*, which consisted of a horse-shaped seat mounted on a tricycle-like device.

Horses and other animal forms (plate 10) might be set upon wheels or a wheeled base so that they could be pulled or pushed along the floor or ground (plates 11 and 12). This basic design served for many different types of transportation, including wagons, ships, trains, automobiles and even airplanes. As each of these phenomena appeared on the world scene, it was faithfully reproduced in wood for the amusement of the small fry.

COLORPLATE 7

COLORPLATE 8

9

10

9.
Rocking horse, carved and painted pine. Still popular with youngsters, rocking horses originated in pre-Christian times. Swiss, dated 1793. New-York Historical Society, New York City

10.
Kiddie-car in the form of an American eagle. Wood, saw-cut, carved and painted. Made by the S. A. Smith Manufacturing Company of Brattleboro, Vermont, this is a rare example of a common toy. American, 1900–20. Margaret Woodbury Strong Museum, Rochester, New York

11.
Horse pull toy, carved and painted wood. Pull and push toys are simple to make and simpler to use, and have a long history in the child's world. American, New York, early nineteenth century. New-York Historical Society, New York City

12.
Pull-toy man and horse, incorporating a whistle, wood carved and painted. American, Pennsylvania, late eighteenth century. Museum of the City of New York

11

12

13.
Jumping jacks, wood, cut, carved and painted. *Left to right:* Soldier, American; Puss-in-Boots, English; bear, Russian. All nineteenth century. A toy of great antiquity, the jumping jack appears throughout the world. Museum of the City of New York

Wooden toys can also be animated by hand or by use of a spring. In the former category we find jumping jacks and various figures that are stick-mounted. The jacks, which move about when strings attached to their extremities are pulled, are of Oriental origin, but have been made all over Europe and the Americas (plates 13 and 14). Stick-mounted toys come in diverse forms. Some of the animals appear to climb a tree or a ladder, while others (chickens and various birds) peck at the ground in search of food.

Spring-motivated devices include the jack-in-the-box and squeak toys. Jack-in-the-boxes were once known in Europe as Punch boxes—a reflection on the fact that the traditional type contains a clownlike figure with a peaked cap, believed to be based on the figure of Punch from the medieval Punch and Judy show (colorplate 9). However, such boxes may also contain snakes and other animal forms.

Squeak toys (plate 15) consist of a wooden or papier-mâché animal, usually a bird, which is fixed to a thin piece of wood above a small bellows. Pressing down on the animal or the board causes the bellows to emit a squeak, somewhat like a cat or bird's cry. Widely made in

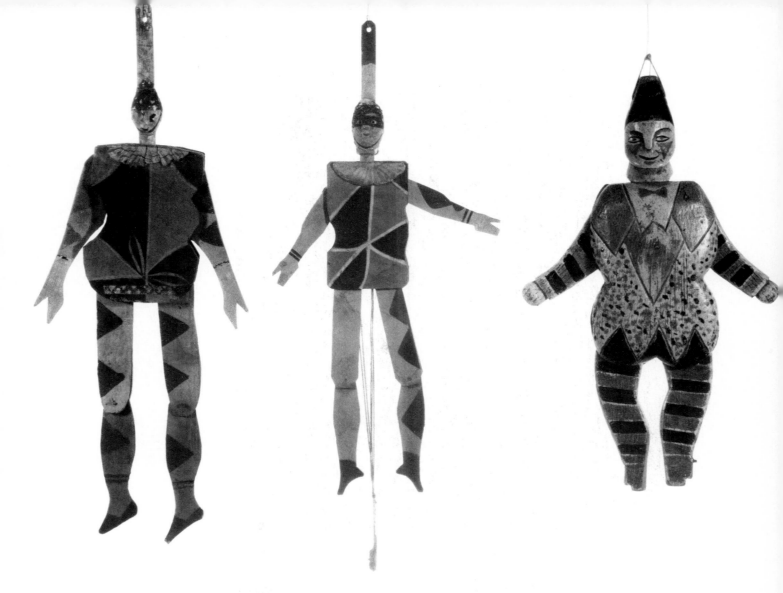

14.
Jumping jacks, wood, cut, carved and painted. Although it appears in many forms, the jumping jack is best known in the guise of a clown. European, early nineteenth century. New-York Historical Society, New York City

15.
Squeak toy, composition, with wood and cloth base, painted gray. Once popular, squeak toys, because of their fragile nature, are now rare. European, c. 1910. Margaret Woodbury Strong Museum, Rochester, New York

Colorplate 9.
Jack-in-the-box, wood and composition, carved and painted, with a wire, cloth-covered spring. Although the traditional jack-in-the-box figure is that of Punch, other figures or animals may be substituted. German, c. 1915. Margaret Woodbury Strong Museum, Rochester, New York

Colorplate 10.
Horse-drawn trolley pull toy, lithographed paper on wood. Lithography allowed for more rapid and less expensive decoration than the traditional hand painting. R. Bliss Manufacturing Company, Pawtucket, Rhode Island. American, c. 1895. Margaret Woodbury Strong Museum, Rochester, New York

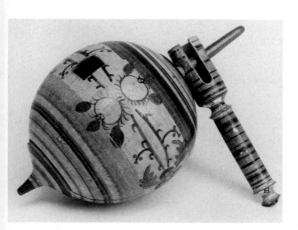

16.
Top and grip, wood turned and painted. Tops of various types have long been popular in Europe and North America. European, late nineteenth century. Museum of the City of New York

the Sonneberg area of Germany, and in Pennsylvania, these play-things were so fragile that only a limited number have survived, but their frequent appearance in nineteenth-century portraits would indicate that they were once rather common.

There were many other simple yet extremely popular wooden toys. Hoops, which came in a dozen sizes, might be rolled along the ground or flung back and forth between players who caught them on sticks. Hoops (which were also made of metal) were known to the ancient Egyptians and Greeks and appear in early paintings, including *Kinderspiel* by the Flemish painter Pieter Breughel the Elder (c. 1520–1569). In eighteenth-century France, hoop playing was considered conducive to the development of grace in young ladies. In the United States during the nineteenth century it became something of a passion; the hoop was thought of as a "patriotic toy," often decorated with thirteen stripes, or, lacking these, a like number of notches.

Also very popular, particularly by the second half of the nineteenth century, were stilts, tenpins and tops. Although made of various materials, tops were most often wooden—the better examples being shaped from lignum vitae or another durable wood and brightly painted. Some tops were propelled by being whipped along with a piece of leather, while others came equipped with a wooden grip to assist in casting them (plate 16). Late in the nineteenth century tin tops, which hummed when they spun, appeared on the market.

Most early wooden toys were primarily handmade, but by the middle of the last century factories on the Continent and in the United States were turning out large numbers of standardized, mass-produced playthings. These included building blocks (plate 17), puzzles (plate 18) and figural toys. The pieces were usually jigsaw-cut with the use of patterns, and were decorated either by means of stencils or through the application of lithographed paper designs (colorplate 10).

One of the most successful of these businesses was run by Charles M. Crandall of Montrose, Pennsylvania. Charles Crandall (1833–1905) devised the first system of tongued and grooved building blocks, as well as various construction figures—flat wooden forms covered with lithographed decorations (plate 19) that could be assembled to create everything from gymnastic performers (plate 20) to a piece of artillery. An excellent seller was the Treasure Box, claimed in an 1881 note in the *Wide Awake Advertiser* to be "not a single toy, but a dozen in one, comprising a Wagon, Top, Bedstead, 2 Chairs, Wheelbarrow, Mallet, Bench, Table, Puzzle, Set of ABC Blocks, a group of nine Domestic Animals and a pretty Suburban Village. A most delightful combination for the little folks." Things had come a long way from the first wood carvings of the Black Forest.

COLORPLATE 9

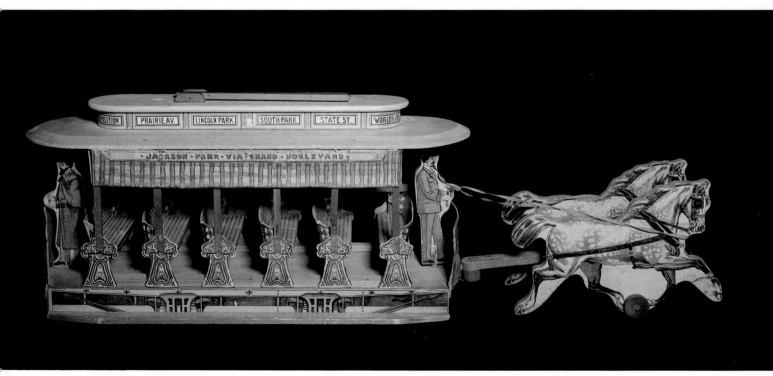

COLORPLATE 10

17

18

17.
Set of building blocks in the form of brownstone houses. The saw-cut wooden blocks are covered with lithographed paper. American, New England, c. 1850–70. Museum of the City of New York

18.
A Mother Goose scroll puzzle, jigsaw-cut wood covered with lithographed paper. Such puzzles first appeared in the sixteenth century, and remain popular today. McLoughlin Brothers, New York. American, late nineteenth century. Museum of the City of New York

19.
Circus wagon, jigsaw-cut wood covered with
lithographed paper. Toys such as this reflect
the nineteenth-century fascination with the
"Big Top." Charles Crandall, Montrose,
Pennsylvania. American, c. 1885. Margaret
Woodbury Strong Museum, Rochester, New
York

20.
Construction blocks — "The Acrobats" —
turned and jigsaw-cut wood covered with
lithographed paper. Charles Crandall, Montrose, Pennsylvania. American, c. 1867–90.
Margaret Woodbury Strong Museum,
Rochester, New York

4 Dolls, Dollhouses and Playthings

Dolls and Related Toys Although it is reasonable to assume that human beings would choose to comfort and amuse their offspring with small likenesses, we know almost nothing about the earliest history of dolls. Medieval writings, however, point clearly to the existence of dolls, and by the 1400s the English were already importing French dolls dressed in the latest Parisian fashions. The best known of their own early dolls are those of the Queen Anne period, c. 1700–30: carved wooden figures with jointed, pegged-on arms and legs, extraordinarily high foreheads and large, rather vacant faces. Equipped with human hair and painted features, Queen Anne "lady" dolls (colorplate 11) were exported to the Americas during the late eighteenth and early nineteenth centuries.

Peg dolls, cruder wooden forms, were made in Holland at about the same time. Ranging in size from an inch to a little over a foot, these clothespin-shaped figures were often termed "Dutch dolls." An English version took the name of "penny wooden," reflecting the fact that it was typically sold for a single copper.

The peg form is very old, and appears in Asia and Africa as well as in Europe. In Japan there is the *Kokeshi* (plate 21), a turned wooden figure with a round head and a body that can be realistically carved or merely painted to give the semblance of form and clothing. The Kokeshi have been sold at temples and during street fairs for hundreds of years, and remain popular today. As with most Japanese dolls, there are regional types, and an expert can tell where a doll was made merely by examining its costume and hairstyle.

Wood was certainly one of the first materials employed in doll-making, and it is still in use. The medium does not necessarily have to be crude. Extremely fine carved dolls and marionettes have been made in Europe. In the East the Japanese have proven particularly adept at sculpting everything from royalty, fishermen and store-keepers to Sumo wrestlers (colorplate 12).

Colorplate 11.
Queen Anne–style "lady" doll, carved and painted wood. Queen Anne dolls are among the earliest of the British and European dolls, but the number of surviving examples indicates they were made in large quantities. English, eighteenth century. Margaret Woodbury Strong Museum, Rochester, New York

21.
Pair of *Kokeshi* dolls, wood, carved and painted. Simple folk dolls such as these are traditional gifts for Japanese children on "Girls' Day." Japanese, late nineteenth century. Private collection

Other early materials included bone and leather, which were employed by the American Indians, and corn husks, a popular medium on the American frontier, where children often grew up never seeing a factory-made doll. Typical corn-husk dolls had tassel hair, hand-painted faces and a short life span (plate 22).

Since most dolls are customarily clothed, the portions of the body most evident and most appealing to the child are the extremities and especially the head. Carved wooden heads can reach a high degree of sophistication, but such work takes time and is expensive. As a result, dollmakers have used a variety of materials to create heads and to a lesser extent limbs.

Dolls with heads made out of wax first appeared in the eighteenth century. Soft and pliable, the wax could be easily cast in molds, and when tinted it had an almost unearthly realism. Despite its obvious fragility, wax remained a popular medium for doll heads throughout much of the nineteenth century. Some of the finest examples were made in England, particularly in the shops of the Marsh and Pieroti families. The French and the Germans also made dolls with wax heads (plate 23), though of a somewhat inferior quality.

Colorplate 12.
Sumo wrestlers, wood, carved and painted, with human hair; background tent in silk and wood. The skillful carving of these toys reflects a long tradition of folk art. Japanese, late eighteenth to early nineteenth century. Kyoto National Museum

COLORPLATE 12

22

23

24

22.
Doll in nineteenth-century dress, corn husk, steel pins and wire. Although made in other countries, corn-husk toys are thought of as particularly American. Midwestern United States, late nineteenth century. New-York Historical Society, New York City

23.
Doll with wax head, composition body and printed cloth dress. Made by Dressel, Cuno & Otto, a major German manufacturer, this doll is typical of factory-produced wax-headed dolls. German, c. 1863–95. Margaret Woodbury Strong Museum, Rochester, New York

24.
Jointed doll, tin head, wooden arms and legs. Although somewhat fragile, painted tin added a lifelike quality to dolls. American, c. 1820–40. New-York Historical Society, New York City

Colorplate 13.
Child doll, bisque head and extremities, cloth body. The French firms of Jumeau (the maker of this doll) and Bru dominated the bisque-doll field throughout the nineteenth century. French, c. 1880. Margaret Woodbury Strong Museum, Rochester, New York

25.
Mechanical doll on a tricycle: composition body clothed in printed fabric; tricycle and spring-wound mechanism in metal. Wind-up dolls of this sort usually had cheap composition or celluloid bodies. American, late nineteenth century. New-York Historical Society, New York City

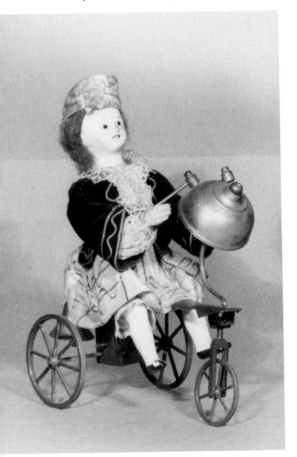

Tin was another material popular for dolls' heads, especially among the larger factories, which often obtained their heads from individual tinsmiths. The material could be cut or shaped by hand; it was then decorated either with stencils or by a process of lithography, or freehand. American dolls in this medium usually have stuffed cloth bodies and carved wooden arms and legs (plate 24).

Clay has been utilized to make complete dolls (or portions of their bodies) for hundreds of years—some of the earliest-known doll-like figures are in this medium. Sun-baked clay was used in Pre-Columbian South America, in Africa and in the American West; in Europe, kiln-fired earthenware was employed. Tiny dollhouse figures were often made in this way, and clay heads are found on some larger dolls.

Porcelain, though, proved to be more popular with most Continental manufacturers. Molded porcelain heads, hands and feet could be glazed or painted to achieve a remarkably lifelike appearance and were inexpensive to produce. In the nineteenth century glazed doll elements came to be a profitable sideline for such German porcelain makers as Meissen and Dresden, which sold them in quantity to local doll manufacturers to be combined with cloth or kid bodies.

By the nineteenth century, Germany had become a leading exporter of porcelain-headed dolls. But France proved a worthy rival. The French factory owners, such as Jumeau (colorplate 13) and Bru, preferred the muted texture of unglazed porcelain or bisque: for collectors, French bisque-headed dolls are now among the most desirable and expensive of all toys. Characteristically, bisque dolls were elaborately detailed, with natural hair and realistic eyes and teeth. Many came equipped with a handsome selection of custom-made clothing. Although porcelain-headed dolls were made elsewhere on the Continent and in the United States, the high quality and large volume of the German and French firms enabled them to control the field and to ship their products throughout the Western world.

Another material widely used in the manufacture of doll heads and other components was composition, which might consist of various ingredients, including sawdust or plaster dust mixed with water and an adhesive. Like porcelain, composition could be molded and painted to achieve a lifelike appearance (plate 25), though in quality it could not compare with the more expensive material. Its durability and lower cost led to its continued use in the making of the cheaper grades of dolls.

Papier-mâché (many layers of paper mixed with glue and water, molded to shape, then later painted) was known in the fifteenth century and was used in furniture making before being employed in doll manufacture. German factories pioneered the making of papier-mâché-headed dolls, but one of the most successful innovators in this field was an American, Ludwig Greiner of Philadelphia, who patented the process in 1858.

26.
Baby doll, soft rubber, painted. Since the rubber deteriorates rapidly, few early rubber-bodied dolls have survived. Italian, c. 1860. Cooper-Hewitt Museum, gift of Mrs. James Russell Soley

Colorplate 14.
Mechanical, or animated, doll, tin, wood and cloth. Called "Daughter of the Regiment," this clockwork doll was made by the well-known Ives, Blakeslee & Company of Bridgeport, Connecticut. American, c. 1876. Margaret Woodbury Strong Museum, Rochester, New York

Colorplate 15.
Automaton, composition, wood, metal and cloth. A man with the head of a monkey, this animated figure once poured a glass of wine. French, nineteenth century. Cooper-Hewitt Museum, gift of Rodman A. Heeren

Rubber and celluloid have also been used. The first rubber doll appeared in America soon after 1850; within a decade similar dolls were being made in Europe (plate 26). But rubber dolls did not really come into their own until the turn of the century, when more anatomically minded parents and children found them ideal for a doll that was to be frequently fed and bathed. Celluloid was invented in 1870 and, like composition, it had the virtue of being cheap to produce. Celluloid dolls are fragile and not particularly attractive. For the most part, the use of this material has been confined to small figures of mediocre quality.

Whatever material they might be made from, most dolls are more or less alike in appearance and purpose; however, certain types do stand apart. There are animated dolls, which walk, push a carriage or ride a bicycle (plate 25 and colorplate 14). The first of these appeared in the 1820s, but again they have a very long history dating back to ancient Greece, where Daedalus supposedly created moving statues of the gods, and Hero of Alexandria is said to have employed waterpower to activate figures of men and beasts.

During the sixteenth century clockmakers turned their skills to the manufacture of animated figures, and in the following centuries French, Austrian, German and Swiss manufacturers produced these *automata*, as they are termed, in substantial quantity. Automata were hardly toys. Powered for the most part by finely made clockwork motors, they were intended primarily for the amusement of adults and were always quite expensive. Monkeys (colorplate 15), clowns and human figures are among the examples to be found today. Sand-powered automata (plates 27 and 28) are more common and less complex than the spring-driven examples; they are also generally less interesting.

The development of animated dolls proceeded slowly. Even though one had been developed by 1820, it was not until the 1850s that a Frenchman, Alexandre Nicholas Theroude, designed a model that could be produced inexpensively enough to make it practical as a toy. Related developments were dolls that opened and closed their eyes (again first appearing in the 1820s), and a phonograph doll, which was patented in 1878 by Thomas Alva Edison (1847–1931).

Other dolls noted for their unusual appearance rather than for anything they do are the pedlar doll and the fortune-telling doll. The former appeared in England in the eighteenth century, and remained popular for more than one hundred years. Usually made of wood and dressed in the costume worn by a working woman of the period, the pedlar doll had a variety of tin cooking utensils or other objects pinned to its ample skirts (plate 29). Fortune-telling dolls were similarly made, but had pieces of paper containing handwritten fortunes pinned to their skirts (plate 30); they thus combined the functions of doll and game. Yet another specialized type was the fashion doll

COLORPLATE 14

COLORPLATE 15

27

27.
Sand-powered automaton or sand toy, lithographed paper and wood. Pouring sand down a chute causes the musicians to appear to play. Made by Gerard Comagni. Italian, c. 1850. Museum of the City of New York

28.
Sand-powered automaton or sand toy, lithographed paper and wood. Although the background for this animated monkey and organ grinder is New York City's City Hall Park, the piece was probably made in France. European, c. 1860–70. New-York Historical Society, New York City

29

30

29.
Pedlar doll, face and hands of painted white kid, clothing and other objects of cloth and tin. Pedlar dolls mirrored the dress and manner of nineteenth-century street merchants. Made by C. & H. White, Milton, Hampshire. English, c. 1820. Margaret Woodbury Strong Museum, Rochester, New York

30.
Fortune-telling doll, wood, carved and painted, cloth and paper. Fortune-telling dolls offered the added attraction of playing the game of fortunes. German, mid-nineteenth century. Margaret Woodbury Strong Museum, Rochester, New York

31.
Stuffed rag "mammy doll," painted cloth face; cast-iron and brass child's stove with brass utensils. Cloth soft toys are among the first owned and most treasured of children's playthings. American, late nineteenth century. Museum of the City of New York

mentioned earlier. These date back to the fourteenth century, but more than five hundred years later such figures were still being shipped from France to acquaint women in other parts of the world with current trends in the fashion capital.

Rag dolls and other soft toys unquestionably have a long history. A rag doll dating to the fourth century B.C. was found in an Egyptian tomb, and the ease with which such pieces could be made from a few inexpensive materials assured their popularity at any time in any culture. Beginning in the early 1800s and until late in the century, the traditional rag doll (plate 31) was made at home by stuffing a crudely cut form with sawdust, rags or even grass. By midcentury manufacturers in America and elsewhere had begun to print colored patterns on cotton so that these could be cut out, sewn together and stuffed. One of the leaders in this field was the Arnold Print Works of North Adams, Massachusetts (1876–1919). Arnold produced story figures like Little Red Riding Hood, as well as various animals such as the dog Tatters (plate 32).

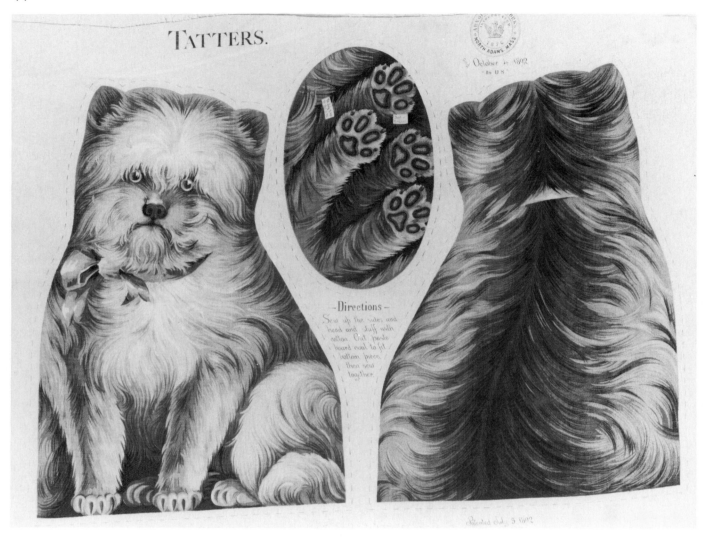

TATTERS.

- Directions -
Sew up the sides and
head and stuff with
cotton. Cut paste-
board oval to fit
bottom piece,
then sew
together.

32.
Pattern for a stuffed rag toy, lithographed
cotton. With the development of lithography, soft-toy manufacturing became big
business. Made by the Arnold Print Works,
North Adams, Massachusetts. American, c.
1892. Museum of the City of New York

It was a far cry from these simple toys to the felt and plush stuffed
toys produced by such well-known makers as Steiff and Lenci. Steiff,
whose products are still being made, started manufacturing its soft
animal figures at Giengen an der Brenz, Germany, in 1879. Lenci,
of Turin, Italy, was established in 1920, and made its name with
sophisticated soft doll figures, hand-painted and designed "for sale
to parents of good taste and distinction." They were also, of course,
expensive.

Steiff was one of the earliest producers of that most popular of all
soft animals, the Teddy bear (plate 33). Inspired by a 1903 Washington *Post* cartoon depicting President Theodore (Teddy) Roose-
velt with a bear cub he had found on a hunting trip, one Morris
Michtom of the Brooklyn-based Ideal Novelty & Toy Company obtained permission to call a stuffed bear he was making "Teddy's Bear."
With its name soon shortened to Teddy bear, the long-nosed, hump-

backed creature was an immediate success. Steiff swiftly got wind of the new animal, and brought out its own version, which sold nearly one million in 1907 alone. The popularity of the Teddy has scarcely diminished over the years. Today, collectors eagerly seek out the earliest examples, particularly those bearing the coveted Steiff mark.

Turn-of-the-century English children had another significant soft toy, a fuzzy black creature known as the golliwog, which was for many years a standard piece of equipment in every nursery. With the development of more sensitive attitudes toward blacks, the golliwog has gradually disappeared, although many examples remain in private collections.

33.
Teddy bear, plush, stuffed with sawdust. During the early 1900s, "Teddies" were owned not only by children but by many young women as well, and sales reached the millions. German, made by the Steiff Company, c. 1910. Margaret Woodbury Strong Museum, Rochester, New York

35

Related to dolls, though serving a somewhat different purpose, are marionettes and puppets (plates 34 and 35). Among the earliest are the shadow puppets (see Chapter 7), which for the most part were cut in silhouette from paper or cardboard. Ordinarily puppets and marionettes were carved in the round or made of baked clay, and were frequently of considerable artistic merit. The Italian pieces are particularly sought after, though the French and the Germans also produced examples of high quality.

Probably no toy has been made or exists today in a variety comparable to that of the doll. It is possible to assemble a collection ranging into the hundreds of examples, even if one concentrates on a single type, such as the bisque-headed doll or the Teddy bear. Small wonder that doll collecting is a leading pastime in the United States, Europe and Japan.

34

34.
Hand puppet, the figure Pantalone, wood, carved and painted, straw and cotton. Puppets, like marionettes, have been used as stage characters since medieval times. Italian or German, early eighteenth century. Cooper-Hewitt Museum, gift of the Estate of Robert W. Chanler

35.
Marionettes, carved and painted wood, glass and cloth. *Left to right:* Harlequin, Columbine, and Pulcinella, all characters who figured prominently in Italian Comedy plays. Italian, eighteenth century. Cooper-Hewitt Museum, gift of Mrs. E. Crane Chadbourne

36.
Dollhouse, wood, lithographed and painted. The furnishings and the building itself are of the period in which it was used. American, c. 1830–40. Museum of the City of New York

Dollhouses and Playthings The first authenticated specimens of dollhouses go back to the sixteenth century. The inventory of a Bavarian estate dated 1581 makes reference to "a big case which contains the dolls' house, in which dolls are to be found in small rooms." Earlier, in 1558, Albrecht V, Duke of Bavaria, commissioned a particularly lavish example with furnishings running into hundreds of items. Although Albrecht purchased the house for his daughter, this piece eventually ended up being displayed in his library—not an unusual occurrence in the sixteenth and seventeenth centuries, when German and Dutch makers created many large cabinet-type dollhouses to be furnished and displayed by adults.

These cabinet houses were just that: large pieces of furniture four or five feet high, often mounted on legs, and generally in the prevailing baroque style. Many had drawers for accessory storage and doors that could be closed to prevent sunlight from harming their delicate contents.

However, there is no doubt that dollhouses were also intended for children. In 1631 Dame Anna Köferlin of Nuremberg had a pamphlet printed describing a dollhouse she had furnished, and setting down the many ways in which the model could serve to instruct young girls in their domestic responsibilities.

Nuremberg was already a major center of dollhouse manufacture, and would remain so for many years. Ulm and Augsburg also produced substantial quantities of such toys; indeed, Germany was pre-

36

Colorplate 16.
Dollhouse, wood, saw-cut and painted, with
furnishings of various materials. By the 1850s,
dollhouses had ceased to resemble display
cabinets and had come to look like contemporary homes. French, c. 1890. Museum
of the City of New York, gift of the Estate
of Louise Wachter

eminent in the field throughout the seventeenth century. By the early eighteenth century, though, Dutch pieces with particularly lavish cabinet work were beginning to attract attention, and the English were entering the field with their "baby houses"—true miniature houses rather than pieces of quasi-furniture.

Still, at this point most dollhouses were really cabinet work and far too expensive even for middle-class children (who no doubt had lesser pieces made by local carpenters or devoted fathers). Not until the nineteenth century did mass-produced houses become available at moderate prices, in England and on the Continent (colorplate 16), and in the United States, which up to then had imported most of its dollhouses.

The earliest-known American dollhouse dates back no further than the period 1744 to 1774; but by the early nineteenth century domestic examples were available in some quantity (plate 36), and after 1850 American designers began to turn out a variety of types. They developed wooden houses decorated with lithographed designs, applied directly to the surface or to paper glued on it, and folding dollhouses of both paper and wood. McLoughlin Brothers of New York City (active 1850–1920) were particularly active in the field of paper houses. In 1894 they patented a "New Folding Doll's House," described in promotional materials as "Designed to be played with on a table. . . . A number of little girls may thus get around it to the best advantage" (plate 37). Another major source of paper houses was the manufacturer Raphael Tuck & Sons of London, founded in 1870.

Dollhouses whether in the United States or abroad were designed in many ingenious ways. Some accurately reflected their owners' homes or an important building in the vicinity; others might be in the prevailing architectural style of the period (plate 38). It was also quite common for manufacturers to continue to reproduce Federal-style houses, for instance, some years after builders had ceased to work in that mode. As a result, it is often difficult to date dollhouses on the basis of style alone.

Simply because they were smaller and often made of less fragile materials, early dollhouse furnishings are found in greater abundance than the houses themselves. The furniture and household accessories deemed necessary for a sixteenth- or seventeenth-century Dutch or German cabinet house often ran into the hundreds. As has always been characteristic of the better dollhouses, these items were designed to match the dwelling and to look as much as possible like their real-life counterparts. Thus, a German townhouse of about 1700 would have a kitchen dominated by a massive fireplace and equipped with tin, iron and brass utensils; its formal rooms would contain lavishly carved furniture, rugs, tapestries and even minute oil paintings.

37.
Folding dollhouse, lithographed paper and cardboard. Patented in 1894, McLoughlin Brothers' collapsible dollhouse was both inexpensive and easy to store. American, c. 1894. Margaret Woodbury Strong Museum, Rochester, New York

38.
Victorian dollhouse, lithographed paper, wood and tin. This elaborate house served as a display beneath the White House Christmas tree in 1978. German, c. 1890. Margaret Woodbury Strong Museum, Rochester, New York

37

38

39.
Rococo revival dollhouse furniture. Desk and armchair in wood, painted and decorated with marquetry; rug in needlepoint. The sophisticated workmanship in these pieces largely predates the era of mass-produced furnishings. Dutch, c. 1840. Margaret Woodbury Strong Museum, Rochester, New York

40.
Dresser, painted cast iron, with glass pulls. Attributed to J. & E. Stevens of Cromwell, Connecticut, this dollhouse dresser was patented in 1867. American, c. 1867. Margaret Woodbury Strong Museum, Rochester, New York

41.
Dollhouse parlor set, stamped and painted tin. This rococo-style suite is painted in imitation of rosewood and is adorned with green flocked upholstery. Attributed to Stevens & Brown of Cromwell, Connecticut. American, c. 1869. Margaret Woodbury Strong Museum, Rochester, New York

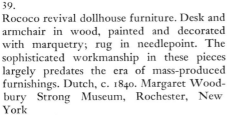

42.
Dollhouse furniture, lithographed cardboard. These pieces were made for the Dunham Manufacturing Company of New York City and were intended to advertise its coconut products. American, c. 1892. Margaret Woodbury Strong Museum, Rochester, New York

This concern for accurate detail continued through the eighteenth century, and was especially noticeable in the nineteenth. Throughout the Victorian era dollhouses boasted of furniture, often upholstered, which was made in the prevailing style, be it rococo revival (plate 39), Gothic or Eastlake. Iron (plate 40) and brass furnishings appeared, as did wax flowers under glass and the most up-to-date heating equipment. There were Staffordshire pieces on the tiny mantels, and an 1880s issue of the popular American periodical *The Youth's Companion* notes: "real marble top tables and sofas in imitation ebony and gold upholstered in terry."

From the middle of the nineteenth century, large toy manufacturers in Europe and North America produced a variety of durable metal furnishings (plate 41), as well as wood and paper ones (plate 42) in the prevailing styles. Later, in the 1920–30 period, Art Deco items appeared on the market.

Colorplate 17.
Child's model butcher shop, wood, carved, painted and stained, and glass. Small-scale representations of shops and street stalls were often sold at fairs and on other festive occasions. English, c. 1800. Cooper-Hewitt Museum, gift of Maude K. Wetmore

43.
Toy Nuremberg kitchen, tin and various other metals, set in a wooden framework. The more elaborate of these kitchens would contain dozens of metal, wooden and ceramic implements. German, c. 1867. Museum of the City of New York

Related to dollhouses are toy kitchens and their accessories, which in some instances were intended to be played with by children, though in others they were strictly for display. In the former category are the so-called Nuremberg kitchens. Set in a three-sided, floored structure, generally made of tin, these models accurately reflected a seventeenth- or eighteenth-century German kitchen. There was a fireplace or stove, pots and pans, stoneware crocks, and even a coal scuttle in the corner (plate 43). Made in Germany for several hundred years, the pieces were shipped throughout the Western world and are often hard to distinguish from similar examples made in England and the United States (plate 44) during the nineteenth century.

Finally, there are the various toy shops and fair stalls, among them bakers', cobblers', milliners' and butchers' establishments (colorplate 17). The more expensive shops were executed in great detail, with the use of polychromed, carved wood, metal and cloth.

Fair or bazaar stalls, some of which were owned by the French Dauphin as early as 1696, include those of broom sellers, flower

dealers and fruit merchants. These were usually less detailed and more crudely made, perhaps reflecting the fact that they were to be sold as inexpensive mementos of village fairs or festivals. In many cases the items in these displays are glued into place and cannot be removed or played with.

In the second half of the nineteenth century most of these more elaborate kitchens, stores and the like were replaced by wood, cardboard or even folding paper grocers' shops distributed by the larger toy manufacturers (see Chapter 7).

Before the nineteenth century it was often difficult to distinguish the dishwares made as toys from those intended as miniatures, collecting of which was an adult hobby. As early as 1779, though, one English commentator was referring to a toy set as "being not quite so small as for baby things nor large enough for grown ladies"; and throughout the succeeding century English and Dutch factories turned out a variety of porcelain and earthenware dishes—generally smaller versions of those being used by adults (plate 45).

Pottery was the usual material, but tea sets were also made in tin and in pewter or Britannia metal (plate 46). As with porcelain, many such services were exported to the United States, which produced little in this field prior to the 1880s.

44.
Toy Nuremberg-type kitchen, wood, cut and painted, furnished with ceramic, tin and brass objects. American, late eighteenth–early nineteenth century. Metropolitan Museum of Art, New York, Sylmaris Collection, gift of George Coe Graves, 1930

45

46

45.
Children's dishware, blue and white Delft with Oriental shapes and decoration. Even in the eighteenth century, "playing house" often presumed a table set with smaller versions of adult pottery and porcelain. Dutch, nineteenth century. Margaret Woodbury Strong Museum, Rochester, New York

46.
Children's tea sets: *left*, Britannia Ware; *right*, tin. For the child whose family could not afford fine pottery, there were always the cheaper and more durable metals. *Left*: English, c. 1865–70. *Right*: American, c. 1860–80. Museum of the City of New York

Kitchenware too had long been popular. As far back as 1800, Georg Hieronymus Bestelmeier (at work 1793–1825), a Nuremberg toymaker, was listing pots, pans and kettles of brass, copper, tin, cast iron and wood in his catalogue. Bestelmeier also made iron stoves, as did the well-known firm of Märklin in Göppingen (established 1859). However, it was the United States, home of the cast-iron toy, that excelled in this field. Elaborate American stoves (see plate 31, page 43) came equipped with matching cookware and were often designed to hold a real fire.

Metal kitchenwares were manufactured in the early twentieth century in England by such firms as Reka Ltd. of London (c. 1908–30), and William Britain's, far better known for its military minia-

47

48

47.
Washstand and bowl for use with dolls; stand of painted sheet steel; bowl and pitcher of ironstone china. European, c. 1880–1910. New-York Historical Society, New York City

48.
Doll's cradle, pine, walnut and hickory, cut and joined. A wide variety of doll cradles are extant, attesting to the importance of this item in the child's world. American, c. 1870–77. Margaret Woodbury Strong Museum, Rochester, New York

49.
Doll's bed; brass frame with cotton drapery. Suspended on a frame, this bed could be rocked. The doll is a "Bye-Lo Baby," a popular late nineteenth-century American type. American, c. 1880–1915. Margaret Woodbury Strong Museum, Rochester, New York

50.
Doll carriage, wood, shaped and painted with metal fittings and canvas hood. Used in New York City during the nineteenth century, this carriage was made by Jesse A. Crandall of Brooklyn. American, c. 1890–1900. Museum of the City of New York

tures. Other related items designed to introduce the neophyte to the joys of housekeeping included washstands (plate 47), and laundry sets such as the "Dolly's Washing Day" combination produced by Chad Valley of Birmingham (established in the 1820s). The last came complete with tubs, scrub board, clothesline and clothespins. There were also ironing sets, pastry equipment (including rolling pins, pie and cake pans) and a variety of playthings intended for use in caring for dolls.

Among the earliest doll-related toys were cradles (plate 48) and beds. A sixteenth-century woodcut depicts a little girl putting her doll to bed in a wooden rocking cradle. However, the makers of cradles rarely signed their products, and the generally archaic appearance of such toys even in the late nineteenth century often makes it difficult to determine just when or where they were made.

Doll beds are a different matter. These tended to follow prevailing adult styles, and it is possible to find them in Empire and various Victorian modes. Large quantities were made in the Berchtesgaden area of Germany to be exported widely. Most examples are in carved and painted wood, but the French made wicker beds and cradles, and brass (plate 49) was also popular.

The doll carriage was a later innovation, although we know that in the fourteenth century infants and small children were already being pulled about in crude cartlike carriages known as *waynes*. It is likely that smaller versions of these vehicles were used as playthings by children, but not until well into the nineteenth century did recognizable carriages appear. First on the scene was the perambulator,

49

50

which had three wheels, one in front and two farther back, a design reflecting the fact that English law forbade the use of four-wheeled vehicles on the sidewalks. By the 1840s doll-size perambulators were popular playthings for girls. In 1880 the sidewalk ordinances were revised to allow carriages with four wheels, and at this time the now-traditional form appeared.

Doll carriages were made in many different styles, ranging from plain and inexpensive examples in wood and canvas to elaborate ones in wicker or brightly lithographed tin with brass fittings. Like so many other Victorian toys, they were also given fancy names. The 1908 catalogue of Simmons and Company, of Bermondsey, London, lists such models as "The Elysian," "The Elegance" and "The Coracle." In the United States early doll carriages were largely made by small manufacturers, but by the 1870s important toymaking firms such as that of Jesse A. Crandall, located in Brooklyn, New York, had entered the field. The Crandall carriages (plate 50) were sturdy and attractive, and could compete effectively with English and German imports.

Finally, girls were provided with numerous child's size household furnishings, from cupboards (plate 51) to chests of drawers and even living and dining room sets. Some of the most interesting of these are homemade, and if creatively decorated, assume almost the role of folk art. The majority, however, were produced in large factories in the United States and abroad. Like doll beds, they tended to follow prevailing adult styles, and the better-made examples are regarded as prime collectors' items.

51.
Child's doll cupboard, pine, cut and grain-painted. This highly decorative piece is in the Empire style appropriate to the period in which it was made. American, c. 1840–65. Margaret Woodbury Strong Museum, Rochester, New York

5   Tin and Cast-Iron Toys

Tin Tinplate—thin sheets of iron coated with rust-resistant tin—has long proved to be an excellent material for toy manufacture. Light in weight and easily worked and decorated, tin was employed in the eighteenth century for the making of cooking utensils, including the diminutive versions used in dollhouses. However, it was not until the early nineteenth century that what we think of as tin toys first appeared in quantity.

The United States, which had imported most of its playthings up to that time, was a pioneer in this new field. The state of Connecticut was a renowned tinmaking center, and its peddlers of pots and pans were well known along the highways and byways of the new republic. Sometime in the 1820s Connecticut tinsmiths began to make a few simple toys—whistles, bubble pipes and the like—and within a decade substantial manufactories had sprung up. Oddly enough, though, the earliest-documented firms were not in this state but in Pennsylvania, where Francis, Field & Francis was active in 1838. A decade later the Philadelphia Tin Toy Manufactory—as the firm was now called—was reported to be turning out wheeled tin "pull toys" in the form of platform-mounted horses, dogs and livestock.

New York was also an early center, but by midcentury the industry was concentrated in the Connecticut River Valley, where it had ready access not only to the tinmakers but also to the clock manufacturers who provided the mechanisms used in clockwork-animated toys. One of the earliest and most successful of these new companies was owned by George W. Brown, a toy designer, and Chauncey Goodrich, a former clockmaker. Combining their talents in George W. Brown & Co., which opened its doors in 1856 in Forestville, these men became pioneers in the making of clockwork toys, including paddleboats, wheeled vehicles and even dancing figures. In 1869 this firm became Stevens & Brown, with the addition of a former

Colorplate 18.
Clockwork-powered train and station, lithographed tinplate. These pieces were produced by Ives Manufacturing Company of Bridgeport, Connecticut, one of the world's leading train makers during the late nineteenth and early twentieth centuries. American, c. 1907. Margaret Woodbury Strong Museum, Rochester, New York

52

partner from the cast-iron toymaking firm of J. & E. Stevens. Now established at Cromwell, Connecticut, Stevens & Brown continued to turn out a variety of tin toys with an emphasis on wheeled horse-drawn vehicles (plate 52).

Even at this point American toy manufacturers had shown a preference for items that were small-scale versions of the things actually used in society. Thus fire apparatus, carousels (plate 53) and carriages were more or less faithful imitations of those a child might see in the adult world. This custom continued into the era of automobiles (plate 54), trolleys (plate 55) and airplanes, and exists today in the toy industry. However, since manufacturers also frequently reproduced vehicles from an earlier era, appearance alone cannot be used to date a piece.

And of course there were many tin toys not based on an existent prototype. Another early maker of clockwork toys, Althof, Bergmann of New York City (established 1856 by three brothers), was known for its distinctly American hoop toys: human figures or animals set within a metal hoop. Put into motion either by hand or by a spring-wound mechanism, these would roll across the floor to the delight of the young.

Stevens & Brown and the other early New England toymakers were successful in their own ways, but all would eventually yield to the giant of the field, Ives and Company, which was opened in Plymouth, Connecticut, by Edward Riley Ives in 1868, and transferred to Bridgeport two years later. In operation until 1931, when it became part of

52.
Horse-drawn Broadway stage, lithographed tin. Attributed to Stevens & Brown of Cromwell, Connecticut, this toy is typical of pre-1900 tin playthings. American, c. 1870–75. New-York Historical Society, New York City

53.
Carousel, painted tin and cloth. The carousel was a focal point of every country fair, and toy manufacturers found small versions to be good sellers. American, c. 1915. Margaret Woodbury Strong Museum, Rochester, New York

54.
Toy wind-up sedan, tinplate and sheet metal, painted and lithographed. Manufacturers produced many toys modeled directly on adult-world prototypes. American, c. 1925. Margaret Woodbury Strong Museum, Rochester, New York

55.
Toy trolley car, tin and sheet metal. Made by Clark & Boyer, of Dayton, Ohio, this friction toy reflects the American interest in modern modes of transportation. American, c. 1905. Margaret Woodbury Strong Museum, Rochester, New York

the Lionel Corporation, Ives made a great many different kinds of toys. Tin was just one of the materials used, yet in each area Ives excelled. Ives's tin clockwork toys, for example, had motors so powerful they would run an hour on a single winding. Its horse-drawn vehicles were the most accurately detailed, its pull toys the sturdiest. In short, Ives was the best.

There were numerous other American manufacturers of tin toys, producing hundreds of thousands of pieces each year, many of which were shipped abroad. Although some collectors are interested only in examples made during the period 1840–90, which has been called the "Golden Age" of American toys, it is important to be aware of the many fine twentieth-century toys. Particularly interesting are those pieces made between 1920 and 1940 by such firms as Louis Marx (plate 56). While these were primarily mass-produced, with some loss in quality as well as charm, they are important in that they reflect American popular culture as revealed in toys.

Marx and other companies brought out a wide variety of tin wind-up toys based on contemporary movie, literary and cartoon characters (plate 57). Popeye is well represented, as is Mickey Mouse; and the Dogpatch Band is a particularly popular musical toy of the era. Nor did World War II mark an end to production. Collectors

53

54

55

56.
Marx Merry Makers, a tin wind-up toy, painted and lithographed. Louis Marx was a giant of the 1930s toy industry, and his novel creations remain popular with collectors. American, c. 1932. Margaret Woodbury Strong Museum, Rochester, New York

are beginning to recognize the importance of postwar tin toys made in the American-occupied zones of Japan and Germany about 1945–52, as well as the possibilities inherent in the relatively few such toys produced in the United States during the same period.

Most of these later toys have one thing in common: they are generally stamped with a manufacturer's name or trademark, and are therefore identifiable. Prior to 1900 toymaking firms sold their wares through jobbers, and the middlemen, who exercised great influence

57.
Wind-up toys, lithographed tin. *Left:*
Happy Hooligan, by J. Chein & Company,
Harrison, New York, c. 1932. *Right:* Barney
Google and Spark Plug, designed by Billy
Debeck, c. 1928. Tin toys based on comic
strip and movie characters caught the public
fancy in the 1930s. Margaret Woodbury
Strong Museum, Rochester, New York

in the market, would not allow makers' marks on goods since these
might enable retailers to reorder directly at a discount from the manufacturer. Most early toys consequently can be identified only through
reference to existing catalogues, company records or individual histories.

After 1900 the jobbers' power was gradually broken, leading to the
use of trade names and trademarks. European toys, it should be noted,
had long borne trademarks, though rarely complete names of makers.

The European toy industry, although generally in advance of the
United States, seems to have entered the area of tin at a somewhat
later date. It is true that metal playthings had been made in Nuremberg, Germany, in the eighteenth century; and the first mass producer
of tin toys appears to have been Mathias Hess (established 1826), in
Nuremberg—a concern that was making trackless tin trains around the
middle of the last century. But not until the advent of Gebrüder Bing,
also of Nuremberg, in about 1863–65, could Europe be said to have
a serious rival for Stevens & Brown or some of the other American
factories.

Once they had started, however, the Germans proved formidable
competitors. Traditionally, their craftspeople had worked on a cottage
system, with individual toy-guild members and their families making
a limited number of pieces that were then sold to Nuremberg middlemen who arranged for their distribution. Hess, Bing and other, later
manufacturers such as Gebrüder Märklin of Göppingen and Ernst
Paul Lehmann of Brandenburg (established 1881) radically changed

all this. They introduced a form of factory mass production based, in part, on recently adopted methods of cutting and stamping. These, along with changes in decorative techniques, meant that far more toys could be produced by a smaller number of workers.

The new methods of decoration were especially important. Previously, each piece had been painted by hand, which proved both slow and expensive. The introduction of stencils had made things a little faster, but it was the application of *chromolithography* to tin that really revolutionized the industry. Henceforth, before being finally assembled, the great majority of toys would be quickly and attractively decorated by the lithographic process, although even after 1900 some toys were at least partially hand-painted.

After 1880, the German manufacturers rapidly obtained a major portion of the world tin toy market. In part this was due to their sophisticated merchandising techniques, which included an emphasis on replicas of certain vehicles (plates 58 and 59) and the tailoring of toys to suit specific countries. In some cases they would market an object directly related to the history or folk culture of a potential customer. For example, the Nuremberg firm of H. Fischer & Company produced in 1922 a tin version of the "Toonerville Trolley," a comic strip–related toy designed specifically for the United States, the only nation where it would have any meaning.

More often, though, a toy would be made in such a way as to appeal to customers in several places. A Märklin battleship (colorplate 19), for example, might fly a German flag and come in a box with instructions written in German; but the identical toy might also be available with English, American or French flags and instructions in the corresponding language.

The German industry also profited from the fact that it was centered in Nuremberg, with its long tradition of toymaking and toy sales. Foreign sales increased to the extent that by 1900 Germany was exporting fully one third of her toy production to the United States alone, with substantial amounts going elsewhere in Europe.

Other Continental nations proved less successful in their efforts. France had several major factories, including that of Fernand Martin of Paris (established 1878), which turned out as many as 800,000 individual pieces in a given year, and the French experience with automata allowed them to produce a variety of sophisticated clockwork toys, as well as those powered by rubber-band or friction motors. However, unlike the Germans, who sought a broad middle market, the French tended either to make very expensive custom toys (such as the detailed auto models manufactured by Jouets de Paris) or cheap "penny toys," for which the basic material was recycled tin cans and which were therefore too fragile to be shipped any great distance. These factors, combined with less experience in toy merchandising,

Colorplate 19.
Toy battleship, lithographed tin and sheet metal. Manufactured by Gebrüder Märklin of Göppingen, this ship is typical of the large and elaborate tin toys popular in the early 1900s. German, c. 1912. Margaret Woodbury Strong Museum, Rochester, New York

58.
Touring car, lithographed tin with clock-work motor. This one was produced by Georges Carette & Cie of Nuremberg, an important designer of toy cars. German, c. 1910. Margaret Woodbury Strong Museum, Rochester, New York

prevented the French manufacturers from offering any real export competition to the Germans.

Great Britain came late to the field. Prior to World War I, English factories confined their efforts in the category of light-metal toys to wagons, velocipedes and other child-size transport—the so-called strong toys that were normally made from much heavier materials than tin. Then, spurred on by the loss of Continental imports during the war, certain manufacturers such as Chad Valley of Birmingham and Wells of London (established 1923) turned their attention to tin toys. Chad Valley, which had been in business since the 1890s, first made mechanical climbing figures like the "monkey on a stick." Next, it initiated a whole line of vehicles, some of which were spring-powered, while others were intended to be pushed or pulled. Chad also used lithographed tin for a popular line of candy and cookie containers in the form of houses and vehicles. These were employed as advertising devices by English sweets makers and are today popular collectors' items.

Wells, too, manufactured figurines, automobiles, ships and the like. During the 1920s and 1930s English production in this area reached a high level of quality, though it could never compete with the volume turned out by the German and American factories.

Cast Iron Although it has attained great popularity with certain American collectors, cast iron was both a late and a limited medium in the toy industry. European manufacturers regularly made cast-iron wheels and other components for tin or wooden toys, but they rarely cast a complete unit. In the United States, by contrast, cast iron enjoyed widespread usage in the late nineteenth and early twentieth centuries.

It is perhaps no coincidence that this popularity roughly coincided with the greatly increased availability of raw iron that followed exploitation of the great Midwestern ore deposits. Certainly cast-iron toys were for the most part a post–Civil War phenomenon. True, one of the earliest manufacturers, J. & E. Stevens of Cromwell, Connecticut, was advertising iron "Fire Cracker Pistols," or cap guns, in an 1859 catalogue; and we know that earlier tin toy manufacturers were buying wheels, couplings and other small parts from Stevens

59.
Wind-up touring car, lithographed tin, also by Georges Carette & Cie of Nuremberg. German, c. 1910. Margaret Woodbury Strong Museum, Rochester, New York

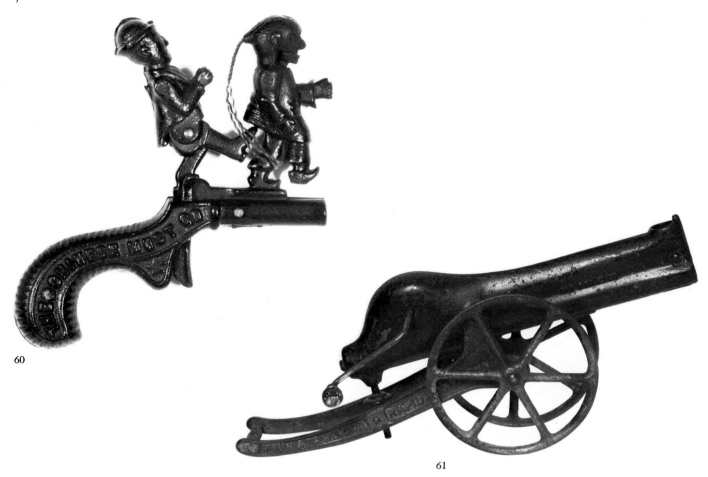

60

61

62

60.
Animated cap pistol, cast iron. When the trigger is pulled, a cap explodes and the Occidental figure kicks the Chinese—a reflection of the hostility to Asians felt in many areas of the United States during the late nineteenth century. Ives, Blakeslee & Company, Bridgeport, Connecticut. American, c. 1890. Margaret Woodbury Strong Museum, Rochester, New York

61.
Toy cannon, cast iron. Described as "the perfect American toy," Campbell's Rapid Fire Gun—as it was known—shot hollow rubber balls. It was made by the Hubley Manufacturing Company of Lancaster, Pennsylvania. American, c. 1911. Margaret Woodbury Strong Museum, Rochester, New York

62.
Bell toy in the form of an eagle, cast iron and steel. Simple in concept but often fanciful in design, bell toys like this one were primarily made by the Gong Bell Manufacturing Company of East Hampton, Connecticut. American, c. 1885. Margaret Woodbury Strong Museum, Rochester, New York

and competing firms. However, it was some years before the iron toymakers could overcome the popularity of the brightly colored and relatively inexpensive tin toys. In the 1860s they began to market still banks and small tools. In the next decade mechanical banks were introduced, to be followed, in about 1879, by a cast-iron train. Not until the early 1880s did vehicles—the most popular of all iron collectibles—become available. The archaic appearance of many of the first examples, due in part to their awkward imitation of contemporary tin models, often leads inexperienced collectors to attribute a much greater age to such toys than most of them warrant.

Once accepted, cast iron proved popular with manufacturers and buyers alike. Gray iron, cast in sand molds, sometimes mixed with brass or lead for greater durability, was not only reasonably sturdy but took paint well and allowed for a uniform product. As methods became more sophisticated, it was possible for a firm to turn out thousands of virtually identical cast figures. The use of standardized parts (the horses on most horse-drawn vehicles are of two or three standard interchangeable types) allowed for economy, and the necessity for hand painting (lithography could not be used) was met by employing a few primary colors in broad, flat areas.

The cap guns were among the earliest pieces made. Some were more or less accurate reproductions of current weapons, but the majority were fanciful "cap exploders" bearing little relationship to a real pistol. Among the most interesting are the animated cap pistols—guns made in the form of a figure that reacts mechanically in some way when the cap is detonated. Such toys are clearly related to mechanical banks and were often made by firms, like Ives and Stevens, that also made banks.

Some animated cap pistols were quite amusing: figures included Punch and Judy, a sea serpent and a monkey with a coconut. There was also the notorious "Chinese Must Go" piece (plate 60), in which the explosion causes an Occidental figure to kick a pigtailed Chinese. Finally there was the usual quota of black figures, Irishmen and other unidentified but abused "furriners."

Related items included cap exploders in the form of cast-iron bombs, in which a cap was placed; when hurled to the ground, the cap would explode on contact. These "bombs" were often in the shape of heads, including those of Admiral Dewey and the Yellow Kid, an early comic strip character. Toy cannons shot hollow rubber balls (plate 61) or exploded firecrackers or small charges of carbide or black powder. Given poetic and often Civil War–related names such as "Yankee" and "Swamp Angel," these remained popular well into the twentieth century.

Another popular early form was the bell toy (plate 62). Although some were clockwork-powered, most of these pieces were intended to be rolled along the floor. As they moved, they gave off a chime or bell tone, or in some cases, such as the "Swan Chariot," a whistling sound. Bell toys came in so many different forms that they can provide the basis of a sizable collection. Some are quite interesting. There is, for example, the optimistically named "Baby Quieter," which kept junior busy ringing a bell while at the same time a figure atop the toy hopped up and down. Also related are the mounted figures, such as Santa Claus (plate 63) and various animals.

All of these cast-iron toys are important to collectors, but when they refer to "iron," they usually mean vehicles, especially the horse-drawn ones produced in such abundance from the 1880s (when the industry really got under way) until well into the 1930s. As in other areas, Ives set the mark to be aimed at (plate 64); but there was substantial competition from such firms as the Hubley Manufacturing Company of Lancaster, Pennsylvania (plate 65); the Kenton Hard-

63

63.
Santa Claus and chariot, cast iron, wood, cloth and cane. Clockwork-powered. German, c. 1900. Margaret Woodbury Strong Museum, Rochester, New York

64.
Firehouse of tin and sheet steel, three-horse fire pumper of cast iron, both by Ives, Blakeslee & Williams, Bridgeport, Connecticut, and patented in 1891. As in many other areas, Ives excelled in the making of cast-iron toys. American, c. 1891. Margaret Woodbury Strong Museum, Rochester, New York

65.
Circus parade wagon, painted cast iron. Made by the Hubley Manufacturing Company of Lancaster, Pennsylvania, which produced various circus-related iron toys. American, c. 1927. Margaret Woodbury Strong Museum, Rochester, New York

64

65

ware Company of Kenton, Ohio (plate 66), which was marketing a line of horse-drawn circus and work vehicles as late as 1952; and Francis W. Carpenter of Port Chester, New York.

Perhaps the most popular of all these vehicles were the fire engines (colorplate 20) and apparatus (plate 67). These came in great variety, from small one-horse chief's wagons to "giant" ladder wagons two feet long drawn by several pairs of horses. The animals were quite standardized, so that identical ones will appear on apparatus used by different firms, complicating an identification problem already made difficult by lack of makers' marks.

Like the tin toymakers, the manufacturers of cast-iron playthings were very much aware of every child's desire to be up to date; and as the vehicle types changed, so did the toys. At first this might merely mean removing the horses from the front of a carriage—a not unreasonable solution at a time when the "horseless carriage" really

Colorplate 20.
Horse-drawn fire-ladder wagon, painted cast iron. Fire apparatus came in great varieties and was very popular with boys. Hubley Manufacturing Company, Lancaster, Pennsylvania. American, c. 1900. Margaret Woodbury Strong Museum, Rochester, New York

66.
Circus bandwagon, painted cast iron. This piece is part of the well-known Overland Circus produced by the Kenton Hardware Company of Kenton, Ohio, and was one of the last original lines of cast-iron playthings. American, c. 1941–52. Museum of the City of New York

67.
Fire-engine pumper, painted cast iron. Elaborate detail and resemblance to contemporary fire apparatus made such a toy especially appealing. American, c. 1885–1905. New-York Historical Society, New York City

looked like just that! However, it was not long before quite accurate reproductions of automobiles, buses, trucks (plate 68) and auxiliary vehicles like motorcycles (plate 69) began to appear on the market. Two of the most prolific manufacturers of these new vehicles were the Dent Hardware Company of Fullerton, Pennsylvania, and the Wilkins Toy Manufacturing Company of Medford, Massachusetts (established 1888). But once again Ives, Kenton and Hubley all kept pace. As the new century dawned, the developing modes of transportation it spawned were imitated in iron.

It should be noted that the majority of these vehicles still lacked mobility. Because of their greater weight, iron toys generally did not

68.
Mack truck, painted cast iron. The introduction of real gasoline-powered vehicles was quickly followed by toys to match. Arcade Manufacturing Company, Freeport, Illinois. American, c. 1930. Margaret Woodbury Strong Museum, Rochester, New York

include the clockwork motors found in many of their tin competitors. Where such a mechanism was used, it was usually designed to operate a subsidiary part of the machine (such as a ladder on a fire truck) rather than to power the vehicle itself. A certain number of iron vehicles were driven by friction motors (plate 70) relying on the release of momentum built up through use of a flywheel; but the larger number were simply push or pull toys.

While land transport predominates, there are also substantial numbers of cast-iron wheeled boats, airplanes, dirigibles and balloons. Although gradually replaced by lighter and cheaper pot metal, and then by plastic, cast-iron toys continued to be made until after World War II.

69.
Motorcycle with sidecar and policemen, cast iron, painted, rubber wheels. Champion Hardware Company, Geneva, Ohio. American, c. 1930. Margaret Woodbury Strong Museum, Rochester, New York

70.
Friction toy, cast iron and wood, painted. Originally designed as a horse-drawn carriage, this and similar vehicles were modified to reflect the introduction of the gas engine. Clark & Boyer, Dayton, Ohio. American, c. 1905. Margaret Woodbury Strong Museum, Rochester, New York

Trains Few toys evoke the nostalgic response elicited by the sight of a toy railway train. Since their appearance in the early nineteenth century, real trains, and especially their steam engines, have stood for progress and a previously unknown freedom of movement; small wonder that as soon as the first railways began to function, diminutive versions appeared. Most of these were intended as models rather than toys. Thus the opening in Germany of the Nuremberg-to-Fürth line in 1835 was commemorated by production of a flat lead casting depicting the little train in all its six-mile-per-hour glory. This model was without power. But only three years later a steam-driven example was exhibited at the Mechanics' Institution in Leeds, England, and by the 1840s relatively sophisticated brass and steel steam engines were being made in Great Britain and North America and on the Continent.

Some readers may be surprised to know that American manufacturers were producing electric trains as early as the 1840s. These, however, proved expensive to make and complex to operate, and would not be able to compete effectively until the end of the century. There were many early unpowered trains that could be pushed or pulled about the room. The French made a variety of such *carpet runners* (so called because they did not operate on a track) during the period 1860 to 1880; and German shops in the Nuremberg area were making brightly painted wooden trains in midcentury.

Not all trackless trains lacked power. Some were steam-driven

71.
Toy locomotive, steam-driven and made of brass. Named *Flying Dutchman*, this engine was made by the Clyde Model Dockyard at Glasgow, Scotland. British, c. 1885. Margaret Woodbury Strong Museum, Rochester, New York

(plate 71), while others relied on friction or the dangerous camphene or burning fluid used in contemporary lamps. But it was the application of clockwork that revolutionized the toy train industry. In 1856 George W. Brown & Co. of Forestville, Connecticut, produced the first clockwork-driven train. Since it was made of tin, it was light enough for the locomotive and several cars to be operated by the power of a single spring. And, equally important, it was far less expensive than the current steam-driven models. For

72.
Toy trackless train, lithographed tinplate with cast-iron wheels. Before the development of rails, toy trains were run on any flat surface, hence the term *carpet runner*. Note that this train is unpowered. American, c. 1870. New-York Historical Society, New York City

the first time it was possible to mass-produce reasonably priced trains.

Although tin was widely used in American trains (plate 72), it was not as popular in Europe, partly because Continental manufacturers continued to prefer the steam-powered trains (plate 73) that required more substantial construction. German manufacturers were producing clockwork trains of tin by the 1880s (plate 74). Some of the better-known makers were located in Germany, where Bing, Märklin, and Karl Bub (plate 75) came to dominate the field.

Bing started making trains in 1882, producing sheet-steel carpet runners and sophisticated steam engines. The firm was one of the first to see the possibilities inherent in encouraging men and boys to collect groups of trains and accessories (known today as "layouts"). During the early 1900s they circulated a periodical entitled *The Little Railway Engineer*, which offered advice and tips on setting up one's own system. This vogue was greatly assisted by Gebrüder Märklin of Göppingen, which produced the first standardized tinplate tracking in 1891, and a year later came out with the figure-eight track layout. Märklin was making electric trains before 1900, and its steam engines were of extremely high quality.

Both Bing and Märklin were major exporters of toy trains, often producing highly accurate reproductions of contemporary American

73.
Steam-powered toy locomotive, brass and tinplate. Though somewhat dangerous to operate, steam engines were the most realistic of toy train engines. German, by Georges Carette & Cie of Nuremberg, c. 1920. Margaret Woodbury Strong Museum, Rochester, New York

75.
Clockwork-powered toy train, lithographed tin with cast-iron wheels. This train was produced by Karl Bub of Nuremberg, one of the more important of the European toy train manufacturers. German, c. 1920. Margaret Woodbury Strong Museum, Rochester, New York

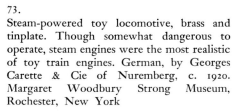

74.
Two clockwork-powered toy trains, both tinplate, painted and lithographed. Train station and accessories of lithographed tin, wood and steel. German, c. 1890. Museum of the City of New York

and British engines and rolling stock. French manufacturers such as C. Rossignol and M. Radiguet of Paris, although they turned out good steam and pull-toy trains, had a relatively small share of the export market. Selling European-made train sets in the United States was not that easy, for domestic manufacturers reached a high level of sophistication at an early date. Brown's clockwork tin trains were quickly followed by others, produced by such major toymakers as Althof, Bergmann of New York City and, of course, Ives (colorplate 18, page 60). The latter was making tin trackless trains in the 1870s, some of them incorporating automatic air whistles and smokestacks belching clouds of real smoke (courtesy of a lighted cigarette).

In keeping with their supremacy in the cast-iron toy field, American manufacturers applied this medium to trains as well. In 1879, Jerome B. Secor of Bridgeport, Connecticut, patented the first cast-iron train set. During the period from 1880 to 1900, Ives and other cast-iron toy producers such as Carpenter (plate 76) and Hubley turned out many examples in this medium. Of course, because of their weight, most of these were still unpowered carpet runners.

Then, in 1884, Murray Beacon patented the first practical electric train. By the end of the century, electrically powered sets had become predominant in the United States and in Europe, where Märklin sold the first examples in 1898. The great manufacturers of electric trains in the United States were Ives, the Dorfan Company of Newark, New Jersey, and, of course, Lionel (colorplate 21 and plate 77), which entered the field in 1901 and came in time to dominate it. Comparable producers overseas were Märklin, Karl Bub (1851–1967) and Frank Hornby of Liverpool, England, whose firm was producing trains in 1920 and is still in operation.

76.
Unpowered trackless toy train, cast iron. Because of their weight, nearly all cast-iron trains were designed to be used as pull or push toys. Made by Francis W. Carpenter of Port Chester, New York. American, c. 1885. Margaret Woodbury Strong Museum, Rochester, New York

77.
The *Flying Yankee*, an electrically powered toy train, tinplate. Made by the Lionel Corporation of New York. American, c. 1935. Margaret Woodbury Strong Museum, Rochester, New York

Colorplate 21.
Electric train, lithographed tinplate. During the 1900s electric trains came to dominate the market, and one of the greatest names in the business was the Lionel Corporation of New York, maker of this set. American, c. 1927. Margaret Woodbury Strong Museum, Rochester, New York

6   Soldiers

To many contemporary enthusiasts, toy soldiers are military miniatures, prized for their exactness of detail and dress. Yet to children, soldiers are still toys, and it has apparently been that way for a long time. As we saw earlier, the existence of the toy soldier is well established by the medieval period, with contemporary woodcuts depicting young men playing with mounted knights (seemingly made of wood), while literary references indicate that metal figures were being manufactured in thirteenth-century Magdeburg.

By 1578 the business had already become extensive enough to require regulation by the Council of Nuremberg. Though certainly also used as toys, these early figures often served a more crucial purpose, being employed in "war games" by kings and generals. Such early strategy sessions would lead eventually to the highly organized replaying of famous battles and wars so popular among collectors of these military pieces today.

Since men of wealth and consequence were involved, it is not surprising that some of these early toys were somewhat out of the ordinary. Louis XIII of France had an entire field army cast in silver, and Louis XIV gave his son a battalion in fine German porcelain. But these were the exceptions. Most early figures were probably of wood, which is still employed in making toy soldiers. Wooden soldiers (plate 78) are either hand-carved in the round or cut out with a jigsaw. In each case they may be hand-painted, and the flat, saw-cut type may also be decorated by direct lithography or by application of lithographed paper.

Because of their fragility, pottery and porcelain figures have never been made in quantity for commercial sale, though some of the ancient examples are in this medium, as are many of the finest, one-of-a-kind showcase examples prized by nineteenth- and twentieth-century collectors.

78.
Two toy soldiers on horseback, wood, carved, plastered and painted. These pieces are representative of the simple wooden soldiers made and sold throughout Europe during the eighteenth and nineteenth centuries. Probably European, c. 1800. Museum of the City of New York

80

79

79.
Toy soldiers, lithographed paper on cardboard. Produced by McLoughlin Brothers of New York City, those wooden-based figures are typical of inexpensive military toys. American, c. 1910. Margaret Woodbury Strong Museum, Rochester, New York

80.
Toy soldiers made of Elastoline, a composition material. Military figures of rubber, paper or composition have never attained the popularity of the tin soldier. German, c. 1925–35. Margaret Woodbury Strong Museum, Rochester, New York

Paper, too, has been utilized. Sheets of soldiers to be cut and assembled were produced by such major toy firms as McLoughlin of New York City (plate 79) and Raphael Tuck of London. Sold at a few pennies per sheet, these brightly lithographed figures presumably offered poorer children the opportunity to amass a sizable military force. Not surprisingly, relatively few of these early paper soldiers have survived their campaigns.

During the first two decades of this century the Grey Iron Casting Company of Mount Joy, Pennsylvania (established about 1904), offered a line of cast-iron soldiers; other manufacturers made soldiers of hard rubber or composition (plate 80), materials that proved impractical, usually because they could not be molded or painted in a sufficiently realistic way.

So it turned out that the thirteenth-century artisans of Magdeburg were right. The most satisfactory medium was lead or a lead alloy. By the early 1700s, small factories in Coburg and Nuremberg, Germany, were producing a sizable quantity of lead soldiers. These were cast in shallow molds engraved by skilled artists, and are now called *flats* to reflect their lack of rounded form. They were hand-painted and generally represented accurate portrayals of troops involved in current campaigns.

The most advanced of the eighteenth-century manufacturers was Johann Gottfried Hilpert, sometimes called "the father of the toy soldier," who worked at both Coburg and Nuremberg. Hilpert was the first to utilize a form of mass production, assigning a group of women to paint a single color on each figure as it was passed from hand to hand. He also issued one of the first catalogues in this field; and, most important of all, made the first efforts to standardize sizes

80

81.
Toy soldiers, cast lead. Made by Heinrichsen, these figures are of the nearly two-dimensional type known as flats, and are dressed in the uniforms of Swiss infantrymen. German, c. 1890. Museum of the City of New York

82.
Hollow-cast lead figures, "The Royal Coach of England." This set was manufactured by William Britain of England, the first successful producer of hollow-cast miniatures. Britain's, as the firm became known, produced thousands of different lead pieces. English, c. 1930. Margaret Woodbury Strong Museum, Rochester, New York

in a field where previously figures might vary between two and ten inches (five and twenty-five centimeters). Hilpert's agreement with certain other makers to produce only soldiers five to six centimeters in height opened the way to collectors who wished to amass large numbers of troops from various sources.

By the end of the eighteenth century, German manufacturers were turning out tens of thousands of "tin soldiers" each year. Many of these were intended for export (though other countries such as France, Denmark and Switzerland had competing factories) and were faithful reproductions of troops serving in the armies of the lands to which they were exported.

Business increased in the nineteenth century. By the 1840s, another maker from Nuremberg, Ernst Heinrichsen (plate 81), had obtained more or less universal agreement on the present standard height of thirty millimeters. At this time some of the German manufacturers could boast of owning as many as five or six thousand different molds for casting lead figures, which might include circus pieces, trees, houses, cannons and related items as well as soldiers.

The French had also been early pioneers in the field, experimenting even in the sixteenth century with fully rounded, three-dimensional figures. Known as *solids*, these pieces were certainly more realistic than the flats, but they were also more expensive and could not compete on the market. Best known of the French firms is Mignot of Paris, which was founded in 1825, and which has produced thousands of highly accurate renditions of historical and military figures. Although it too made flats, Mignot refused to give up on three-dimensional figures, and it was primarily the competition of this firm that forced the German makers reluctantly to move into the area of solid and semiflat (slightly rounded) figures.

Until the end of the last century, flats and the more expensive solids competed for the toy enthusiast's patronage. Then in 1893 William Britain of London revolutionized the field with the introduction of hollow-cast figures (plate 82). Lighter and cheaper than solids, far more realistic than flats, hollow figures proved to be the sign of the future. By the 1900s Britain's Ltd., as the firm came to be called, was

exporting its wares throughout the world—even to Germany, home of the toy soldier. The company reluctantly switched from lead to plastic in the 1960s, but Britain's has produced so many different lead figures over the past decades that its products are still readily available to collectors. They are characterized by great accuracy in sculptural detail and in painting, and represent military and civilian personnel throughout the world.

The United States has produced lead miniatures, some at an early date (plate 83), though most were made during the period between the two world wars. J. L. Wright, Inc., of Chicago (1910–43) made solids for use with its Lincoln Log set, a popular construction toy of that era; and several manufacturers turned out hollow-cast models of American troops (plate 84). These were an inch (2.5 centimeters) or so larger than their European contemporaries and lacked their sophistication in molding and decoration.

Today's children have to be content for the most part with plastic soldiers, which will also no doubt become collectible in time. Their fathers meanwhile continue a long tradition in collecting the world's most sophisticated military miniatures—hand-crafted and hand-painted examples that would make Louis XIII blanch with envy.

83.
Model of Robert Fulton's steamboat, the *Clermont*, cast lead. Lead miniatures were being made in the United States in the nineteenth century, but there was no substantial domestic production until the 1930s. American, c. 1820–30. Museum of the City of New York

84.
Hollow-cast toy soldiers, painted lead. During the 1930s, several firms in the United States manufactured lead soldiers. These were generally larger than their European counterparts and sometimes had stamped steel helmets. American, c. 1930–40. Margaret Woodbury Strong Museum, Rochester, New York

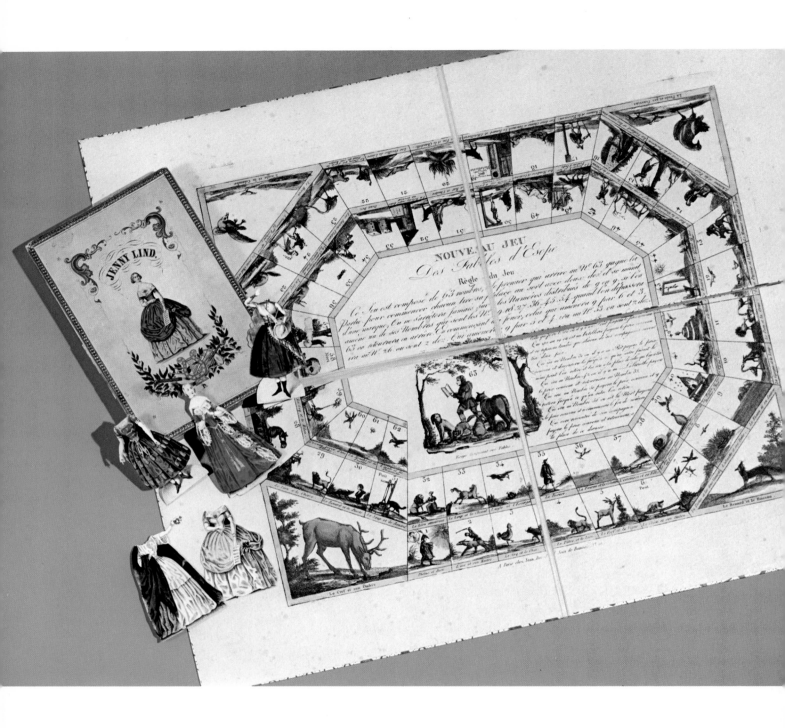

7   Paper Playthings

For the child, as for the collector, paper toys have obvious advantages and disadvantages. They can be mass-produced from inexpensive materials, and therefore sold in large quantity at a very low unit price. But they are the most fragile of toys, and few survive their initial owners.

An amazing variety of paper playthings has been turned out over the past few hundred years. Perhaps the most ancient are shadow puppets: jointed, stiff paper or cardboard figures, which can be manipulated before a light to cast moving shadows and create a convincing pantomime. Such pieces were being made in Asia hundreds of years ago. The first ones known in Europe came from China, where they were the basis of a highly sophisticated form of theater.

The earliest European manufacturers were in Germany, where Georg H. Bestelmeier, a maker of marionettes and puppets, produced his "Chinese Shadow Play," and in Italy. The French were also active in the field at an early period; their articulated figures were often used to tell traditional tales such as that of *Don Quixote* (plate 85).

Somewhat related are *pantines*: cardboard dancers dressed in gauze and gilt, with movable limbs controlled by strings. Made in France during the eighteenth and early nineteenth centuries, these figures were so popular with young women that they were banned by law in certain areas in the odd belief that playing with them might lead to an unwanted pregnancy!

Paper dolls—or dressing dolls, as they are known in England—and their accessories are the most common and the most popular of all such ephemera. Although paper dollhouse furniture was made in Germany at an early date, the English manufacturers produced the first true paper dolls—cutout figures with changeable costumes—in the late eighteenth century. Soon France, where the toys were used to provide inexpensive fashion illustrations, and then Germany entered

Colorplate 22.
Left: Paper dolls representing the singer Jenny Lind and some of her many stage costumes, chromolithographed paper. American, mid-nineteenth century. *Right:* Board game, "The Fables of Aesop," engraved and hand-tinted cardboard and paper. French, mid-nineteenth century. Cooper-Hewitt Museum: dolls, gift of Mrs. Frederick Rosengarten; board game, gift of Hamill and Barker

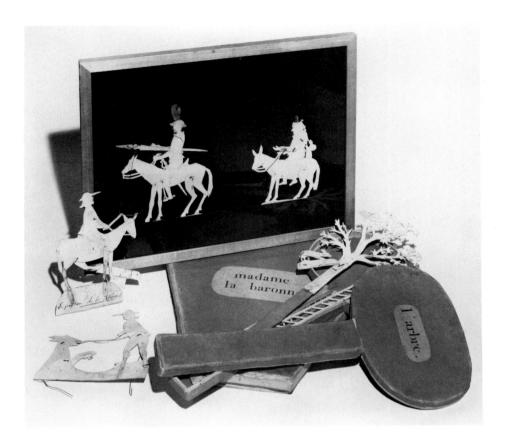

85.
Shadow puppets, articulated figures cut from cardboard. Many traditional tales were told at fairs and other gatherings with the help of these puppets. The two figures at the rear are from a version of *Don Quixote*. French, c. 1800. Cooper-Hewitt Museum, gift of Erskine Hewitt

the field; by 1850 the dolls were being made all over Europe and North America. Normally, the little figures, their costumes and accessories were printed and sold in sheets that could be cut apart and assembled. Most types were available both colored and plain, the latter selling at a considerable discount in addition to allowing the young owners to exercise their discretion as to style and color. The oldest decorated dolls were engraved and then hand-tinted (plate 86), but stencils and eventually chromolithography were introduced in the nineteenth century, allowing for more rapid and less expensive production.

Paper dolls are the most topical of toys, offering a survey of current styles and popular public figures. As female fashions changed, so did the dolls; and the appearance of a new actor, a gifted dancer or a popular singer—such as Jenny Lind (colorplate 22)—would be sure to set the presses humming.

The major English producer of dressing dolls was Raphael Tuck, a German who settled in London in 1866 and who became, by the 1890s, one of the world's best-known manufacturers of paper toys and games, with offices on the Continent, in New York City and in Sydney, Australia. Although he turned out the usual topical and fairy-tale figures, Tuck also had a line of English kings, princes and princesses and assorted historical characters.

The first known American maker was Crosby, Nichols and Company of Boston, which turned out a well-dressed young lady named

Fanny Gray in 1856. By the 1880s the business was largely in the hands of the big toy producers like McLoughlin Brothers of New York City and Milton Bradley of Springfield, Massachusetts (established 1860). These firms produced many different lines of dolls: some were elaborate and costly; others, the "penny-a-sheet" variety, were inexpensive enough to be afforded by almost everyone. There were even free or almost-free paper dolls. Certain business firms gave these away or included them with a small purchase as an advertising gimmick (the firm's name and its message usually appeared somewhere on the doll). And there were the cutouts that appeared regularly in women's magazines such as *Godey's Lady's Book*, *McCall's* and *Woman's Home Companion*. These most accurately reflected current clothing styles.

Nor were the young men forgotten. Some of the earliest toy soldiers were made of paper; and from the early nineteenth century on, the firm of Pellerin at Épinal in France produced remarkably detailed paper construction sheets from which airplanes and submarines (plate 87), railway stations and even entire villages might be

86.
Paper dolls, watercolor on paper. Although such paper figures appeared in the eighteenth century, they were so fragile that few early examples survive. American, mid-nineteenth century. New-York Historical Society, New York City

made. In the United States such firms as Milton Bradley (which supplemented its lines of paper dolls and doll furnishings with paper trains and sidewheel steamers) followed suit.

Among the most interesting of all paper toys are the theaters. These originated independently in Germany and England. In both cases they were initially based on figures representing current actors and productions, which were made for the amusement of adults. Around 1800, the stiff paper and cardboard theaters were provided with wings so that they could stand alone, and children were offered the opportunity to reenact popular plays.

Credit for first popularizing such toys goes to the firm of J. F. Schreiber of Esslingen, Germany (active c. 1810–1914). First engraved, then lithographed, these theaters and their figures were sold in sheets to be cut apart and assembled. The English producers were especially prolific in putting out several versions of every current production from 1820 until the 1870s, when juvenile interest began to wane.

One English publisher of toy theaters, Benjamin Pollock (1856–1937), continued to work into the twentieth century, and his business is still carried on today under different management. In 1884 Robert Louis Stevenson "discovered" Pollock's and wrote an article about the business for an influential periodical, *A Magazine of Art*, which revived the toy theater industry and greatly enhanced the firm's reputation. Pollock's lithographed theaters are attractive (see frontispiece), and he is particularly important in that he purchased the rights to, and then reproduced, many early plays previously owned by defunct publishers.

The first American toy theaters did not appear until the 1870s, long after they had ceased to be a novelty on the Continent and in England. The earliest-known example is "Seltz's American Boy's Theatre," which was sold by Scott & Company of New York City for twenty-five cents plain and twice that in color—a far cry from the one or two pence the early English manufacturers asked for their considerably more elaborate examples. And, of course, the larger U.S. firms followed suit as well, with McLoughlin turning out a variety of theaters in the 1880s and 1890s.

Many of the more intricate toy theaters were built up in layers to create the illusion of depth achieved on the actual stage by the use of flats. In this respect they are somewhat related to the earlier perspective toys known as peep shows (see Chapter 9).

87.
Construction sheets, lithographed paper. During the nineteenth and early twentieth centuries, the French firm of Pellerin produced a variety of sheets like these, which could be cut and pasted to create vehicles, animals and buildings. French, c. 1900. Museum of the City of New York

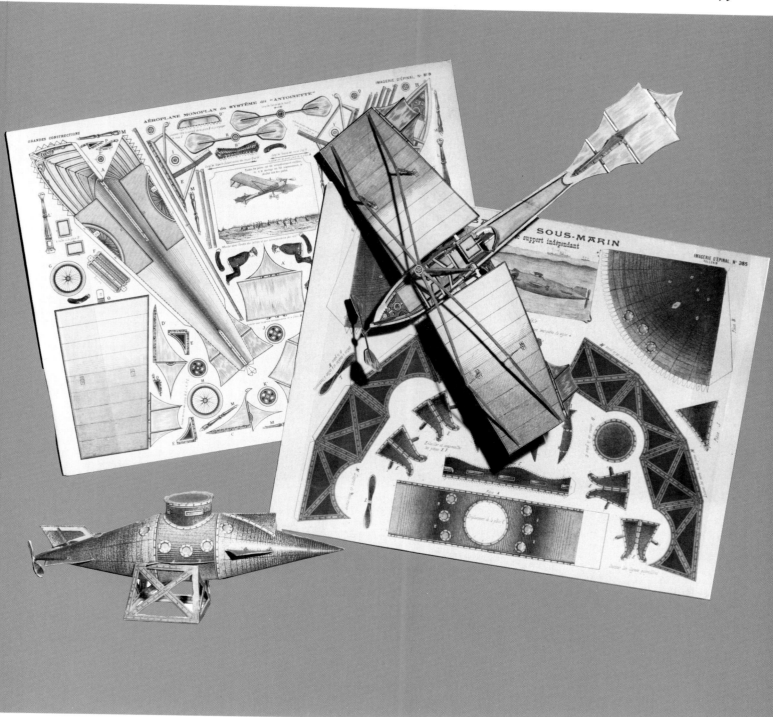

8   Card, Table and Board Games

Even in the busiest and most hectic of times there have to be some quiet interludes. Both children and adults have traditionally occupied such moments with a variety of card, board and table games. The most ancient of such amusements appears to have been playing cards. Their use in Europe can be traced back to the Middle Ages, and they are believed to have existed in China at an even earlier date.

A fourteenth-century English manuscript illustration shows a king and two of his courtiers engaged in playing a card game with cards that look remarkably like the modern version, and the household accounts of Charles VI of France for the year 1392 list expenditures for playing cards. But the pastime was clearly not confined to royalty; indeed it appears to have been so widespread as to create serious social and moral problems. The German city of Regensburg outlawed their use in 1378, and the provost of Paris issued an edict in 1392 limiting the occasions for card playing.

Although card playing has long been associated with gambling and various evil pastimes, it can serve purposes other than the exchange of funds among participants. As early as the sixteenth century, monks were being instructed in their duties through the use of specially designed cards; and in Germany, where playing cards were manufactured from the beginning of the fifteenth century, educational cards were produced by 1603. In England also, where decks of cards first appeared in 1463, a set of playing cards designed to teach the rudiments of mathematics, "The Scolers Practicall Cards," was issued by 1656. In the nineteenth century inexpensive, factory-made cards were covering subject matter ranging from current literature (plate 88) to geography, grammar and botany. It was not until midcentury that this predominant interest in education and training was replaced by one directed more toward pleasure and family

Colorplate 23.
Board game, "The Animal Kingdom" ("Die Thierwelt"), hand-colored wood engraving on stiff paper in a marbleized paper and cardboard slipcase. Graphic design and bold colors attract many collectors to board games. Austrian, Vienna, c. 1835. Cooper-Hewitt Museum, gift of Hamill and Barker

Colorplate 24.
Chessmen, wood, painted in polychrome gouache. The chess pieces represent the protagonists in an early nineteenth-century military conflict in the Tyrol. Austrian, early nineteenth century. Metropolitan Museum of Art, New York, gift of Gustavus A. Pfeiffer, 1948

88.
Playing cards, thin cardboard, lithographed in black and white. Gambling with cards dates to at least the medieval period, and cards appear to have been made in substantial quantities from 1800 on, for a wide variety of nineteenth-century cards is available. This pack illustrates scenes from Charles Dickens's novels. American, c. 1885. Cooper-Hewitt Museum, gift of Jean McKinnon Holt

amusement. Humorous games such as "Dr. Busby" and "Rook" began to appear, providing a lot of fun leavened with just a bit of learning.

The earliest playing cards were hand-drawn and -colored, but by the 1600s stencils and engraving were already being utilized to create more or less uniform and substantially less costly decks. The invention of lithography in the nineteenth century led eventually to mass-produced cards. These remain sufficiently common that most enthusiasts collect them by the pack, while earlier cards are uncommon enough to justify the accumulation of odd cards.

Board games have an even earlier lineage than playing cards. They have been found in Egyptian tombs, and chess, checkers and backgammon can all be traced back into the earliest epochs of human history. Chess, the sport of kings, has long been regarded as the preeminent strategic game. In accord with this high status, chessboards are often elaborately decorated with inlay and the addition of precious metals and jewels (plate 89). Chessmen are even more likely to be lavishly designed, frequently carved in the shape of historical personages, mythological beasts or military figures of a certain period (colorplate 24). Backgammon, which is undergoing a current revival, has long been popular; and checkers, as the game of the common man, was often contested on attractive folk-painted boards.

89.
Folding chess and Tric Trac board and box, walnut inlaid with copper gilt, ivory, mother-of-pearl, serpentine, rosso antico marble. As the game of kings, chess was often played on elaborate surfaces. Spanish, Castile, c. 1518–56. Metropolitan Museum of Art, New York, Pfeiffer Fund, 1963

90.
Board game, "The Prefectures of France,"
lithographed paper on cardboard. Although
intended primarily for pleasure, board games
could, as in this case, serve as educational
tools. French, mid-nineteenth century.
Cooper-Hewitt Museum, anonymous donor

91.
Board game, "The Mansion of Happiness," lithographed paper on cardboard. Many board games carried a religious or moral message. This game was produced by Thayer & Company, Salem, Massachusetts. American, c. 1850–65. Margaret Woodbury Strong Museum, Rochester, New York

Today, the term *board game* generally refers to one involving a race to the finish line between two or more contestants whose movement along a predetermined course on the board is governed by the spinning of a dial, the turn of a card or the casting of dice. Depending on the complexity (and cost) of the game, accessories will include the board, counters and such additional items as paper money and prize cards.

The earliest known of such games is "Goose," which was being played in sixteenth-century Italy. German children were soon enjoying similar amusements, and by 1759 Carrington Bowles of London had produced the "Journey Through Europe or the Play of Geography," one of the first of many educational board games. The British also patented "Roman History," while French children learned of their own country through "The Prefectures of France" (plate 90) or took a lesson in morality from "The Fables of Aesop" (see colorplate 22, page 90), and Austrians studied "The Animal Kingdom" ("Die Thierwelt"—colorplate 23).

At first, religion and morality were stressed even more heavily than book learning. "The Game of Pope or Pagan or the Siege of the Stronghold of Satan by the Christian Army," manufactured in 1844 by W. & S. B. Ives of Salem, Massachusetts, is perhaps the best known of the religious board games; but there were others, such as "The Mansion of Happiness" (plate 91), "The Cottage of Content or the

92.
Board game, "The District Messenger Boy," lithographed paper on cardboard. This game for the upwardly mobile was produced by McLoughlin Brothers of New York City, one of the most prolific makers of board games. American, c. 1910. Margaret Woodbury Strong Museum, Rochester, New York

Right Roads and Wrong Ways," put out in 1848 by William Spooner of London, and "The Swan of Elegance" (John Harris of London, c. 1815), a story of childish tribulations whose hero was a boy named Zealous Peter.

By the second half of the nineteenth century, a new morality became dominant—one based on material success. Games professing to show the way to Heaven were superseded by such pastimes as "The Game of Business or Going to Work" and "Speculation for Young Children"; while for those of more humble beginnings there were Horatio Alger–style rags-to-riches games, such as "The District Messenger Boy" (from office clerk to company president in fifty easy moves; plate 92). As befitted her expanding economy and growing corporate wealth, the United States produced the bulk of these "money games." The ultimate in such activities was "Monopoly," which was patented in 1935 by Parker Brothers of Salem, Massachusetts, the same firm that had produced "The Game of Business" and "Speculation" way back in 1895. But Parker Brothers hardly had a "monopoly" on the games field. As noted previously, W. & S. B. Ives also manufactured board games during the late nineteenth and twentieth centuries, as did McLoughlin Brothers and the famous Milton Bradley Company of Springfield, Massachusetts, which is still turning out games.

The earliest board games were engraved and hand-decorated just like playing cards, but by the 1830s, when lithography was being employed, the traditional paper "boards" were replaced with cardboard playing surfaces. Almost from the beginning brightly colored boxes and playing surfaces were the rule, probably because they attracted more customers. For today's collector, the graphic design of these elements is of paramount importance, though the fact that most such games are marked and dated by their manufacturers is also very appealing.

What have been called *table games* constitute the third category in this chapter. Dominoes are one of the oldest and best known; there were numerous other similar pastimes, many of which are now known only from the elaborate ivory counters used in playing them (colorplate 25). "Pick Up Sticks" (known as "Spillikins" in England), and several versions of table skittles (a game in which a wooden ball is rolled at tenpin-like figures) have existed for at least two centuries, as have various types of rolling and tossing games (plate 93). The Victorian era saw a proliferation of small versions of outdoor sports. The most popular of these is Ping-Pong, but there were also copies of croquet, golf, baseball, soccer and even fox hunting. Many games involved setting up large, rather complex courses or fields of play, and came with a variety of accessories from rackets, balls and nets to tiny figures. Few of the older versions are ever found in complete condition.

Colorplate 25.
Game counters and storage boxes: ivory counters, hand-colored; boxes of ivory, each bearing a figure representing a continent—Asia, Africa, Europe and America. Designs engraved by Julius Goltzius after drawings by Martin de Vos (1532–1603). French, late seventeenth century. Cooper-Hewitt Museum, gift of the Trustees of the Estate of James Hazen Hyde

Another category would encompass those games that are in the nature of puzzles and involve solving problems. Some entail disengaging wooden or metal objects, while others are color-related (plate 94). Despite the inroads made by radio and television (now, like most other modern developments, themselves the subject matter of board games), game playing continues to be a popular pastime. The contemporary examples will be grist for the collector's mill in the not-too-distant future.

93.
Beanbag toss game, lithographed paper on wood. The goal of the game is to throw the beanbags through the trapdoor-like openings surrounding the figures' heads. R. Bliss Manufacturing Company, Pawtucket, Rhode Island. American, c. 1905. Margaret Woodbury Strong Museum, Rochester, New York

94.
Puzzle-type board or table game, "Flora, das Blumenspiel," colored engraving on paper with colored wooden chips. This game falls somewhere in the area between true puzzles and construction kits. German, c. 1830–35. Cooper-Hewitt Museum, gift of Hamill and Barker

9   Optical Devices

Ever since the first cave dwellers amused their offspring (and themselves) with shadow figures cast on firelit cave walls, human beings have been fascinated by the possibilities of sight. Eventually this would lead to the development of cinema, but movies were preceded by a variety of devices that are generally known as optical toys, most of them developed for the amusement or edification of adults. Only after they had ceased to be a novelty to this audience did they truly become children's playthings—often in a simplified or less expensive form.

The first optical devices were extremely simple. As far back as the fifteenth century, pictures cut out and folded in the manner of a concertina were expanded and then viewed through a small hole in a wooden or cardboard box (plate 95). These *peep shows*, as they were called, created a perspective image of some depth (plate 96). The earliest examples were drawn and colored by hand, but by the nineteenth century it was possible to obtain sets of lithographed peepshow views illustrating famous locations such as Westminster Abbey and historic events like the Battle of Waterloo.

Somewhat similar in nature, though lacking the illusion of depth, was the Myriopticon, manufactured in the mid-nineteenth century by the Milton Bradley Company of Springfield, Massachusetts, which consisted of a group of Civil War scenes wound on rollers so that a continuous panorama of the Great Rebellion would pass before the viewer's eye as a crank was turned.

From viewing such images to projecting them was a natural step. A Jesuit priest in Germany, Athanasius Kircher, was probably the inventor as early as 1640 of what came to be called the *magic lantern*. This was a metal box fitted with a concave mirror and a lens, behind which a light source was set—initially a candle, later everything from a kerosene lamp to gas or electric lights (colorplate 26). Glass slides

Colorplate 26.
Magic lantern, glass lens, painted and stamped tin body. The ability of the magic lantern to project an image fascinated every early audience and frightened some. French, second half of the nineteenth century. Cooper-Hewitt Museum, gift of Frederick P. Victoria

95

96

on which scenes or figures were painted were drawn slowly across the lens and thus projected upon a wall or other surface. Originally, the slides too were painted by hand, and they consisted of a single panorama that passed before the viewer's eyes. Later, after 1850, most such slides would be photographically produced, and divided into several distinct scenes or tableaus that might or might not be related. The subject matter would vary, with travel, humor and religion among the more popular topics, and so appealing are these slides that they are today regarded as collectibles in their own right.

The process was taken a step further with development of the stereoscope (plate 98), which relies for its three-dimensional effect on the phenomenon of binocular vision. This creates an illusion of depth when the same object is seen simultaneously from two slightly different angles. In 1832 an Englishman, Sir Charles Wheatstone (1802–1875), employed mirrors to create this effect; and the various devices flowing from his efforts are now highly collectible. Most common, of course, are the later stereoscopic photographs and the viewers used with them.

So far, all these instruments produced only a static image. Men of science had long known of vision persistence—the ability of the eye to retain the impression of an object for a fleeting instant after its disappearance. The first device to exploit this human characteristic

95.
Frame-mounted peep show, polychromed wood, brass and glass. Three people could watch a candlelit peep show through the viewing ports of this large stand-up device. French, late eighteenth century. Cooper-Hewitt Museum, gift of Eleanor and Sarah Hewitt

96.
Peep show, steel engraving and watercolor on paper. The expansion of the concertina-shaped peep show creates a feeling of depth and reality. German, mid-eighteenth century. Cooper-Hewitt Museum, gift of Mrs. James Ward Thorne

(which is, of course, at the foundation of motion picture production) to achieve a semblance of motion was the Thaumatrope, developed early in the nineteenth century. It consisted of a circular disc, each side of which bore a related image, such as a sitting boy and a cart. By rotating the disc rapidly, it was possible to make the boy appear to be seated in the cart.

The Phenakistoscope (plate 97) was also invented in 1832. The cardboard discs used in this machine bore a series of drawings, each slightly different from its predecessor. When viewed by turning the discs while looking into a mirror through slots cut next to each figure, an impression of continuous motion was obtained: the first motion picture. An improvement on the Phenakistoscope was the Zoetrope (plate 98), or "Wheel of Life," first manufactured commercially in 1860. A similar strip of slightly variant images was employed, but in this case they were seen through slits in a hollow metal cylinder that spun on a vertical shaft. Originally made in France, the Zoetrope was produced in large numbers by the Milton Bradley Company.

Other optical toys include the Italian Gioco di Luce ("Game of Light"), the kaleidoscope and the anamorphic, or distorted, picture. The first of these (colorplate 27) is a box in which sand poured from above activates a wheel holding a variety of colored discs. Candle-light shining from behind the discs creates the impression of a con-

97.
Phenakistoscope, lithographed paper and wood. Viewing the spinning disc creates an illusion of movement—the first "moving picture." Austrian, Vienna, c. 1832. Cooper-Hewitt Museum, purchased in memory of Mrs. John Innes Kane

stantly changing flow of colors. (There are further sand toys in which the flow of earth activates figures—see Chapter 4—but these are more in the nature of mechanical toys than optical ones.)

The kaleidoscope, invented in about 1817 by a Scotsman, Sir David Brewster (1781–1868), consists of three mirrors fixed in a cylinder containing fragments of varicolored glass. When the tube is turned or shaken, the glass forms attractive geometric patterns that vary constantly with the movement. The better kaleidoscopes were made at least in part of brass, had turning mechanisms and were mounted on wooden stands (plate 98).

Another device known as "Les Anamorphoses," or "Les Métamorphoses," (see colorplate 1, page 6) consists of a series of deliberately distorted pictures which, seemingly by magic, become clear when viewed in a highly polished metal cylinder placed in specific relationship to them. Anamorphic devices are among the oldest of optical toys, dating back at least to the seventeenth century.

Colorplate 27.
Gioco di Luce ("Game of Light"), polychrome wood case, paper and metal. Pouring sand through a chute activates a wheel upon which colored discs are mounted. When lit from behind, the resultant patterns are kaleidoscopic in effect. Italian, Savoy, c. 1780. Cooper-Hewitt Museum, Mary Hearn Greims, George A. Hearn and Misses Hewitt Fund

98.
Optical devices. *Left to right:* Kaleidoscope, glass, brass, cardboard and wood, American, c. 1873; Zoetrope, metal with wooden stand, images lithographed on paper, European, mid-nineteenth century; stereoscope, metal, wood and glass, "The Kinora," English, late nineteenth century. Cooper-Hewitt Museum, purchased in memory of Mrs. Samuel Stiefel (kaleidoscope), in memory of Mrs. E. Henry Harrison (Zoetrope) and in memory of Rodman Wanamaker (stereoscope)

10 Banks

The use of banks (or money boxes, as the English call them), both to encourage savings and to provide a safe place for a child's money, goes back a surprisingly long way. Simple forms have been found in ancient graves, and from sixteenth-century England comes a written reference to boxes made of "potters clay wherein boyes put their money to keepe, such as they have in the shops towards Christmas."

These early banks were made of wood or earthenware, and if of pottery were generally in a simple pear shape, although more elaborate examples were developed in the nineteenth century. Later American and English examples, particularly those from the Lambeth district of London and the county of Staffordshire, often took the form of people (plate 99 and colorplate 28), buildings or small animals. American potters, especially those in Pennsylvania, made equally interesting types, shaping their banks as schoolhouses, chests of drawers, even chickens.

The wooden banks were never as popular as the earthenware ones, perhaps because of their fragility, and fewer examples have survived. Those still extant are frequently painted with bright colors or inlaid in silver, brass or mother-of-pearl. Wooden banks are often dated and bear the name of their owner—a rarity on the ceramic or metal pieces.

There is no doubt that the banks most abundant and most popular with collectors are the tin or cast-iron factory-made types of the nineteenth century. These fall into three categories: still, mechanical and registering banks. The first group, which includes the pottery and wooden models, consists of banks that simply receive and store coins, usually through a slot. The second group comprises those banks in which insertion of a coin triggers some mechanical activity, generally by figures that are an integral part of the money box. Finally, there

99.
Still bank in the form of a human head, glazed earthenware. These banks were made in many different forms, including the humorous or satiric. English, c. 1900. Margaret Woodbury Strong Museum, Rochester, New York

Colorplate 28.
Still bank in the form of the head of an American Indian, earthenware. Simple repositories for money have existed for centuries, the earliest being of pottery or wood. European, c. 1900. Margaret Woodbury Strong Museum, Rochester, New York

are the registering banks, which operate on the principle of a cash register, keeping track of the funds deposited.

The earliest of the mass-produced items were tin still banks. These were probably American in origin, the industry having been given a boost by the chartering of the first United States Savings Bank in 1816. As one might expect, the initial forms were those of safes or bank buildings; by the second half of the nineteenth century manufacturers such as Stevens & Brown of Cromwell, Connecticut, were turning out brightly stenciled or lithographed churches, drums, hats and houses (plate 100).

German makers also came early to the field; English examples did not appear in force until the 1860s, when interest had shifted to banks made of cast iron. These too were at first still banks, but the use of molds allowed for a variety of novel forms. In the United States a multitude of wild and domestic animals now appeared, as did patriotic figures like Uncle Sam and George Washington, and buildings of every kind from cabins to skyscrapers.

Not all banks were mere coin depositories. Some had the additional role of embodying the political satire so popular in the later nineteenth century. The English firm of John Harper & Company (Willenhall, Staffordshire) caricatured the Boer leader Paul Kruger as a squat, ugly dwarf, while General Benjamin F. Butler's candidacy for President of the United States in 1884 on behalf of the Greenback Party was hardly enhanced by a bank portraying him as a frog with one arm embossed "Bonds and Yachts for Me."

Most examples were quite innocent, though. Usually the makers of still banks came closest to commenting on the world around them when they produced pieces in the form of popular cartoon characters like Mutt and Jeff, Buster Brown and Tige, and Little Orphan Annie. Such banks are generally dated after 1900, and are sometimes cast of aluminum or pot metal rather than iron.

Around 1860, manufacturers primarily in the United States began to experiment with iron banks that incorporated figures activated by the deposit of a coin. Between 1880 and 1910, over a thousand different mechanical banks were patented. Some of these, especially the products of J. & E. Stevens, were extremely clever, well calculated to attract the attention of young and old alike. A figure of Uncle Sam might drop a coin into his satchel, while the same principle would be employed in a bank involving a monkey feeding a lion (plate 101) or a horse doing tricks (plate 102). Or the coin might be propelled through the air by pressure on a spring-loaded button, as in the well-known William Tell bank, or stuffed down the throat of an unwilling patient by a zealous dentist. The possibilities seemed limitless.

100.
Still bank, Victorian house of painted tin. This sprightly red, green and blue bank is typical of the novelty types made by firms like Stevens & Brown of Cromwell, Connecticut. American, c. 1880. New-York Historical Society, New York City

101.
Mechanical bank, painted cast iron. A penny placed in the monkey's hand is dropped into the lion's mouth. American, c. 1883. New-York Historical Society, New York City

102.
"Trick Pony," a mechanical bank made of cast iron and patented in 1885 by the Sheppard Hardware Company of Buffalo, New York. American, c. 1885–90. Margaret Woodbury Strong Museum, Rochester, New York

103.
Mechanical bank, "Paddy and His Pig," cast iron, painted. This bank is an example of those toys that poked fun at unpopular ethnic groups. American, c. 1882. New-York Historical Society, New York City

100

101

102

103

Not all the figures portrayed were viewed in a favorable light. Groups in popular disfavor, such as blacks (colorplate 29), Irish and Chinese, were sometimes caricatured in mechanical banks. One of the better-known examples is the "Paddy and His Pig" bank, in which pressure on a button causes a coin balanced on the pig's nose to be propelled into the Irishman's gaping maw (plate 103).

Registering banks, which are found in tin and cast iron, are generally of less interest to collectors. Some—such as the Dime Register, in which the handle of an old-fashioned pump was moved up and down as the amount deposited registered on the top of the well bucket—have an obvious appeal; but most are simply miniature cash registers. One example, Uncle Sam's Coin Register Bank, patented in 1912, was still in production a half century later, setting an unmatched record for longevity in this field.

Banks, particularly mechanical ones, form one of the most popular areas of toy collecting. It is not unusual for a rare mechanical bank to bring a large sum of money at auction. Unfortunately, skyrocketing prices have led to reproduction of some of the most popular old banks (plate 104). Collectors should be aware of this problem and be prepared to do the research necessary to distinguish between old and new pieces.

Colorplate 29.
The "Dark Town Battery," a mechanical bank with a baseball theme—and, like "Paddy and His Pig" in plate 103, an ethnic comment—painted cast iron. This bank was patented in 1888 by J. & E. Stevens of Cromwell, Connecticut, one of the first makers of such toys. American, c. 1890–1900. Margaret Woodbury Strong Museum, Rochester, New York

104.
Still bank in the form of George Washington, painted cast iron. This piece is an accurate copy of a nineteenth-century bank and an example of the hard-to-spot reproductions now in this area. American, c. 1950. Margaret Woodbury Strong Museum, Rochester, New York

104

11 Advice for the Collector

The potential collector is faced with a bewildering variety of choices among antique toys. Not only are there many different categories, ranging from dolls to such relatively esoteric fields as automata and marbles, but in many cases the objects involved have been mass-produced for over one hundred years by numerous manufacturers. However, certain superior items are immediately set apart by their style, quality of manufacture or rarity. A much greater number of relatively mediocre pieces may be collected, particularly by the beginner, but will in the long run prove to have little real value either aesthetically or monetarily.

Collecting should be fun, and it is possible to have a great deal of fun collecting toys. Remember that many of the rules applicable to other areas of antiques apply also to toys. Don't buy what you don't know (unless the price is so low that it's an act of charity to take it away). Either study your area sufficiently to be able to understand what you are being offered, or deal only with sellers who guarantee their merchandise and have a reputation for integrity. As in other types of collecting, such individuals generally charge a premium, so most serious collectors prefer to become conversant enough with the field to be able to find their own bargains.

Admittedly, bargain hunting in the toy field has its particular perils. Because so many of the more popular toys—dolls and cast-iron banks and trains, for example—were made in large quantities in factories, it is possible to obtain examples from which copies may be made; and these reproductions look disconcertingly like the real thing. Mechanical banks are fraught with problems: because the rarer or more attractive examples now bring sums in the hundreds or even thousands of dollars, it has become worthwhile for people to make reproductions, either from existent original molds or from the banks themselves. Properly painted, aged and distressed, such pieces can fool most collectors. Any cast-metal toy can be dealt with in the same manner, so that collectors in the fields of lead soldiers, iron trains and vehicles, and early metal doll furnishings face the same potential danger.

The question of condition is also important. As in all types of collecting, the goal is a piece in new or nearly new condition, with its original paint and no repairs. But most toys are fragile; paint chips or wears off; parts get lost. In some areas, such as doll collecting, enthusiasts may regard it as quite proper to redress a figure, or even to add an original head to a replacement body. So few pristine pieces exist that compromises simply must be made. But those collectors who specialize in tin and cast-iron toys are much more demanding: they object to any repainting and to most repairs. Thus anyone buying a refurbished piece should anticipate some difficulty in selling it for very much.

Again, the golden rule of collecting holds: buy the very best that you can afford. The rare, the better made, the more attractive piece will almost always retain its value or appreciate at a faster pace than the more ordinary piece. To distinguish between the two requires knowledge of the field—knowledge that can come only with research. There are quite a few good books on collecting toys and there are various specialized toy museums (see Reading and Reference and Public Collections). There are also dealers and collectors conversant with the field. All these sources should be made full use of to develop a good background in one's chosen area.

Because toy collecting is so popular, toys are relatively easy to acquire. Most antique dealers handle a few. Pieces are usually available at every show and many auctions, including specialized ones devoted entirely to this field. Examples may also be obtained through advertisements in antiques publications.

Regardless of source, certain examples and certain classifications are likely to remain quite expensive. On the other hand, because the field is so broad, it is possible to find attractive toys that remain underpriced. At present, good bargains can be found in the categories of board games and tin clockwork toys from Occupied Japan and Germany. Optical devices are also presently underpriced and undercollected. New collectors might do better to buy the best in one of these fields rather than paying top dollar for mediocre items in a more competitive area.

Since toys are rarely antiques in the true technical sense of being at least a century old, many can be researched. It is often possible to learn a good deal about a specific item from old catalogues, factory histories and similar materials. This opportunity is one of the greatest inducements for some toy collectors. Even if you do not share such generalized interest, it is often important, particularly when buying an uncommon toy, to have details of where and how it was made.

As in every kind of collecting, the happiest collectors—those who are most pleased with their hobby and their acquisitions—will generally be the ones who have devoted the most time to learning about their specialty, joining clubs and promoting the care and preservation of these important mementos of our past.

Glossary

automata, clockwork or otherwise mechanically driven figures that mimic human movements. They date to ancient times, with some of the finest examples being made in France during the seventeenth to nineteenth centuries.

baby house, a popular English term for dollhouse.

battledore and shuttlecock, a game in which a feathered projectile (the shuttlecock) is hit back and forth with flat bats (battledores). It is of great age, and has been popular in Asa as well as in Europe and North America.

bilboquet (stick and ball), a game in which the player attempts to catch a wooden or ivory ball connected by a cord to a shaft that has either a point or a shallow cup on one end.

bisque (biscuit), unglazed porcelain, commonly used in the making of doll heads, hands and feet in French and German factories of the nineteenth century.

board games, games that are played on a course laid out on a cardboard "board" or surface. Movement is generally dependent on the spin of a wheel, the drawing of a card or the cast of dice.

box toys, toys—construction sets, chemistry sets and the like—that are sold and stored in boxes.

carpet runners, early clockwork, steam or unpowered trains that did not run on a track but simply on a flat surface.

cast iron, iron with a high carbon content that is shaped in molds while in a liquid state. Although brittle, it has often been used in toy manufacture.

chromolithography, lithography in color, achieved by use of several stones or plates, each inked in a single color. Most late nineteenth-century toys were decorated in this way.

clockwork, a wound-spring mechanism commonly used to propel nineteenth- and twentieth-century toys. Such toys are often referred to as mechanical or animated.

composition, a plasterlike material that can be shaped to form and then left to harden. Widely used in the late nineteenth and early twentieth centuries, especially for doll heads and bodies.

flats, metal soldiers or military miniatures that are cast in shallow molds so that they lack depth of form.

friction toy, a weight-driven toy, which is propelled by the inertia obtained from contact between the toy's wheels and a solid surface.

hobbyhorse, various types of playthings that consist of a horse's head or head and body on a stick, and that may be straddled or "ridden" by a child.

jigsaw, a saw with a thin vertical blade that can make intricate cuts and is operated with a reciprocating motion. During the nineteenth century most wooden toys were cut out with a jigsaw, although they might later be hand-finished.

knucklebones, an ancient gambling game, originally played with the knucklebones of sheep.

Kokeshi, turned and carved polychrome wooden figures made in Japan and traditionally sold at temples and shrines and at holiday festivals. Animal, human and mythological figures are found.

lithography, the process of printing by use of a stone or metal plate on which a design has been made in a water-repellent material. Often used in the decoration of early toys, particularly those made of paper and tinplate.

mechanical bank, a coin-storage device, featuring fanciful or humorous figures or devices that move in response to the deposit of coins. Such banks were usually spring- or weight-motivated.

Nuremberg Ware, a term used in the nineteenth and early twentieth centuries to describe wooden toys made in Nuremberg, Germany. Such toys were usually produced in homes or small factories and were inexpensive.

pantines, French jointed paper and cardboard toys of the eighteenth and early nineteenth centuries. As with marionettes, they were first hand-tinted and later lithographed.

peep show, an optical toy consisting of paper or thin cardboard cut in layers of descending size and stretched out in an accordionlike manner to achieve an illusion of depth. Some examples were housed in wooden boxes and viewed through peep holes, hence the term "peep show."

porcelain, a hard, white, translucent ceramic used in the manufacture of better-quality dolls' heads, hands and feet.

pot metal, a lightweight lead-copper alloy used in making hollow ware, such as toy vehicles.

pull toys, toys that are mounted on wheels and may be pulled along by a child; they are not mechanically driven.

push toys (stick toys), toys that a child may push along the floor—usually by means of a stick attached to the body of the toy.

registering bank, a bank, generally of tin or iron, that records the amount of money placed within.

sandcasting, the technique of shaping molten iron by pouring it into molds made of sand. Many iron toys were so manufactured.

shoofly, a child's toy consisting of a seat placed between two flat-cut wooden figures (usually horses) set on rockers.

solids, metal military miniatures cast in molds and of solid construction. They are generally three-dimensional.

stencils, cutout paper or metal patterns used in painting designs on tin, paper or wooden toys. Prior to lithography, stenciling was the fastest and cheapest way to decorate a toy.

still bank, a bank that is simply a storage place for coins. Such banks may come in a variety of attractive forms, including houses, stores and various animals.

tinplate, steel covered with tin to retard rust. Tinplate was used in the manufacture of many toys. The term also refers to mass-produced toy trains.

trackless trains, see *carpet runners*.

velocipede, an early form of three-wheeled child's toy resembling the later tricycle.

wheel toys, toys—such as wagons, kiddiecars and the like—that are mounted on wheels and are usually large enough for a small child to sit in or on.

white metal, mixed alloys of lead, frequently used in making small toys. White metal is lighter than lead but also more fragile.

Reading and Reference

General

ARIES, PHILIPPE. *Centuries of Childhood: A Social History of Family Life.* Translated by Robert Baldick. New York: Alfred A. Knopf, 1962.

CULFF, ROBERT. *The World of Toys.* Feltham, England: Hamlyn Publishing Group, 1969.

DAIKEN, LESLIE. *Children's Toys Throughout the Ages.* New York: Frederick A. Praeger, 1953.

FOLEY, DANIEL J. *Toys Through the Ages.* Philadelphia: Chilton Books, 1962.

FRASER, ANTONIA. *A History of Toys.* New York: Delacorte Press, 1966.

FRITZSCH, KARL EWALD, AND MANFRED BACHMANN. *An Illustrated History of Toys.* Translated by Ruth Michaelis-Jena. London: Abbey Library, 1966.

HERTZ, LOUIS H. *The Toy Collector.* New York: Funk & Wagnalls, 1969.

KING, CONSTANCE EILEEN. *The Encyclopedia of Toys.* New York: Crown Publishers, 1978.

McCLINTON, KATHARINE MORRISON. *Antiques of American Childhood.* New York: Clarkson N. Potter, 1970.

Dolls and Dollhouses

EATON, FAITH. *Dolls in Color.* New York: Macmillan Publishing Co., 1975.

JACOBS, FLORA GILL. *Dolls' Houses in America.* New York: Charles Scribner's Sons, 1974.

————. *A History of Dolls' Houses.* Rev. and enl. ed. New York: Charles Scribner's Sons, 1965.

————, and ESTRID FAURHOLT. *Dolls and Doll Houses.* Rutland, Vt.: Charles E. Tuttle, 1967.

Model Trains and Soldiers

BALDET, MARCEL. *Lead Soldiers and Figurines.* Translated by E. Stanton Russell.

New York: Crown Publishers, 1961.

GARRATT, JOHN G. *Model Soldiers: A Collector's Guide.* London: Seeley Service & Co., 1959.

LEVY, ALLEN. *A Century of Model Trains.* London: New Cavendish Books, 1974.

REDER, GUSTAV. *Clockwork, Steam and Electric: A History of Model Railways.* Translated by C. Hamilton Ellis. Shepperton, England: Ian Allan, 1972.

Other Specialties

BOEHN, MAX VON. *Puppets and Automata.* New York: Dover Publications, 1972.

HILLIER, MARY. *Automata and Mechanical Toys.* London: Jupiter Books, 1976.

PRESSLAND, DAVID. *The Art of the Tin Toy.* New York: Crown Publishers, 1976.

TOLLER, JANE. *Antique Miniature Furniture in Great Britain and America.* London: G. Bell & Sons, 1966.

Some Public Collections of Toys

Collections of toys and games are generally not widely published but fine ones can often be found in regional and local historical societies and folk art museums.

UNITED STATES

Buena Park, Cal.:	Knott's Berry Farm
Chicago:	The Art Institute of Chicago Museum of Science and Industry
Cleveland:	The Cleveland Museum of Art
Dearborn, Mich.:	Greenfield Village and Henry Ford Museum
Denver, Colo.:	Denver Art Museum
Milwaukee:	Milwaukee Public Museum
Newark, N.J.:	The Newark Museum
New York City:	Brooklyn Children's Museum
	Cooper-Hewitt Museum, the Smithsonian Institution's National Museum of Design
	The Metropolitan Museum of Art Museum of American Folk Art
	The Museum of the City of New York The New-York Historical Society
Rochester, N.Y.:	Margaret Woodbury Strong Museum
Salem, Mass.:	Essex Institute
Shelburne, Vt.:	Shelburne Museum
Sturbridge, Mass.:	Old Sturbridge Village
Washington, D.C.:	Smithsonian Institution
	National Museum of American History
	(formerly National Museum of History and Technology)
Williamsburg, Va.:	Colonial Williamsburg

OTHER

Amsterdam:	Rijksmuseum
Basel:	Schweizerisches Museum für Volkskunde
Bath, England:	The American Museum in Britain
Bedford, England:	Bedford Museum
Bodman, West Germany:	Kleines Puppenstubenmuseum
Bologna:	Museo d'Arte Industriale Pinacoteca Nazionale
Cardiff, Wales:	National Museum of Wales, Welsh Folk Museum
Dresden:	Staatliche Kunstsammlungen Dresden, Museum für Volkskunst
Edinburgh:	Museum of Childhood
Essex, England:	Saffron Walden Museum
The Hague:	Haags Gemeentemuseum
Ipswich, England:	Ipswich Museum and Art Galleries
London:	Bethnal Green Museum British Museum Museum of London
	Pollock's Toy Museum Victoria and Albert Museum
Munich:	Puppentheatersammlung der Stadt München
Nuremberg:	Germanisches Nationalmuseum
Ottawa:	The National Gallery of Canada
Paris:	Musée des Arts Décoratifs Musée de Cluny
Seiffen, East Germany:	Erzgebirgisches Speilzeugmuseum
Sonneberg, East Germany:	Spielzeug-Museum
Vienna:	Kunsthistorisches Museum Österreichisches Museum für Volkskunde
Windsor, England:	State Apartments, Windsor Castle (Queen Mary's Dollhouse)

Index

Numbers in *italics* indicate pages on which black-and-white illustrations appear.
Numbers in **boldface** indicate pages on which colorplates appear.

Acknowledgments

Cooper-Hewitt staff members have been responsible for the following contributions to the series: concept, Lisa Taylor; administration, Christian Rohlfing, David McFadden and Kurt Struver; coordination, Peter Scherer. In addition, valuable help has been provided by S. Dillon Ripley, Joseph Bonsignore, Susan Hamilton and Robert W. Mason of the Smithsonian Institution, as well as by the late Warren Lynch, Gloria Norris and Edward E. Fitzgerald of Book-of-the-Month Club, Inc.

The author wishes to thank the following for their kind assistance: Brenda Gilchrist, whose patience, knowledge and good humor made the rough spots smooth; Blair Whitton, David McFadden and Christian Rohlfing, whose comments on the text were of great help; and Ann Adelman, Mary Kay Ingenthron, Neal Jones and Peter Scherer.

Credits